PHOTOBOOTH
-A BIOGRAPHY-

meags fitzgerald

This book was possible
with a tremendous
amount of support
from my sister, Eryn.

I am truly grateful.

PROLOGUE

EDMONTON
CITY CENTRE
-ACTIVE-

As a kid, I had my picture taken in a photobooth a few times. Like everyone, I thought it was fun. Photobooths were everywhere in my hometown of Edmonton, Alberta, Canada.

At the end of the tenth grade, my friend Emily and I took a strip of photos to celebrate our last day of classes. It was June 23, 2003.

Something was different that day.

Something clicked.

Suddenly, all I wanted to do was use photobooths, or go "boothing," as I called it.

I very actively started a collection of photobooth pictures.

2003
By grade eleven, I was known as "the photobooth girl."
I went to a high school for the arts. My friends and I usually spent the lunch hour hanging out in front of our lockers.
Friends would ask to see my collection, and I'd pass it around.
We didn't carry hundreds of photos of ourselves everywhere on our phones.
Social media didn't exist as a concept yet,
I had never used a digital camera.
We were art and theatre geeks. We didn't drink or do drugs and none of us had our driver's license.

When I planned to take many strips, I went out of my way to Millbourne Mall, to use a $2 B&W booth.
We were the characters of my collection.
Our world was reflected back at us through the pictures.
In our little world, taking and looking at pictures was entertainment.
There were four colour booths within walking distance of my school for me to choose from. I didn't know it then, but this was the end of a peak period for the Canadian photobooth company.
Back then, I didn't know about the sensitivity of the industry.

2012

You used to see photobooths all the time in shopping centres, arcades and in bus depots, usually near vending machines, kiddie rides, or a row of payphones.

You still pass by one from time to time, but those are most likely digital photobooths.

For the user, the experiences of vintage and digital photobooths are similar. The big difference is how the photographs are made.

In the industry, vintage photobooths are referred to as wet chemistry booths, chemical booths, or sometimes as dip'n'dunks.

The inside of a chemical photobooth with the back removed.

WILL I EVER FIGURE OUT HOW THIS WORKS?
Photographs
The dip'n'dunk system is the most common system for chemical photobooths.
This is how it works.

STEP 1

The process begins when you insert money.

Most booths accept coins, some accept bills and some now take credit cards.

Today, the average cost for a strip of photos is $4 US.

1940s *Coin plate from an American Model 9.*

1990s *From an Australian booth, still operational today.*

STEP 2

The camera is then cued.

A reel of light-sensitive paper sits on top of the camera box and feeds down into it. The camera has a large revolving shutter which exposes the paper through a lens and set of mirrors.

After four flashes, a feed pulls the paper down. A loud "crchunk" sound tells you that a knife has cut the paper from the reel.

STEP 3

From the camera, the paper slides into an arm of the "spider" which has swung out from the inner cylinder to catch it.

The arm and strip then submerge into a tank and bob there for ten seconds. It repeats in all fourteen tanks.

A photobooth can have up to seven spider arms, so as many as seven photostrips can develop at once.

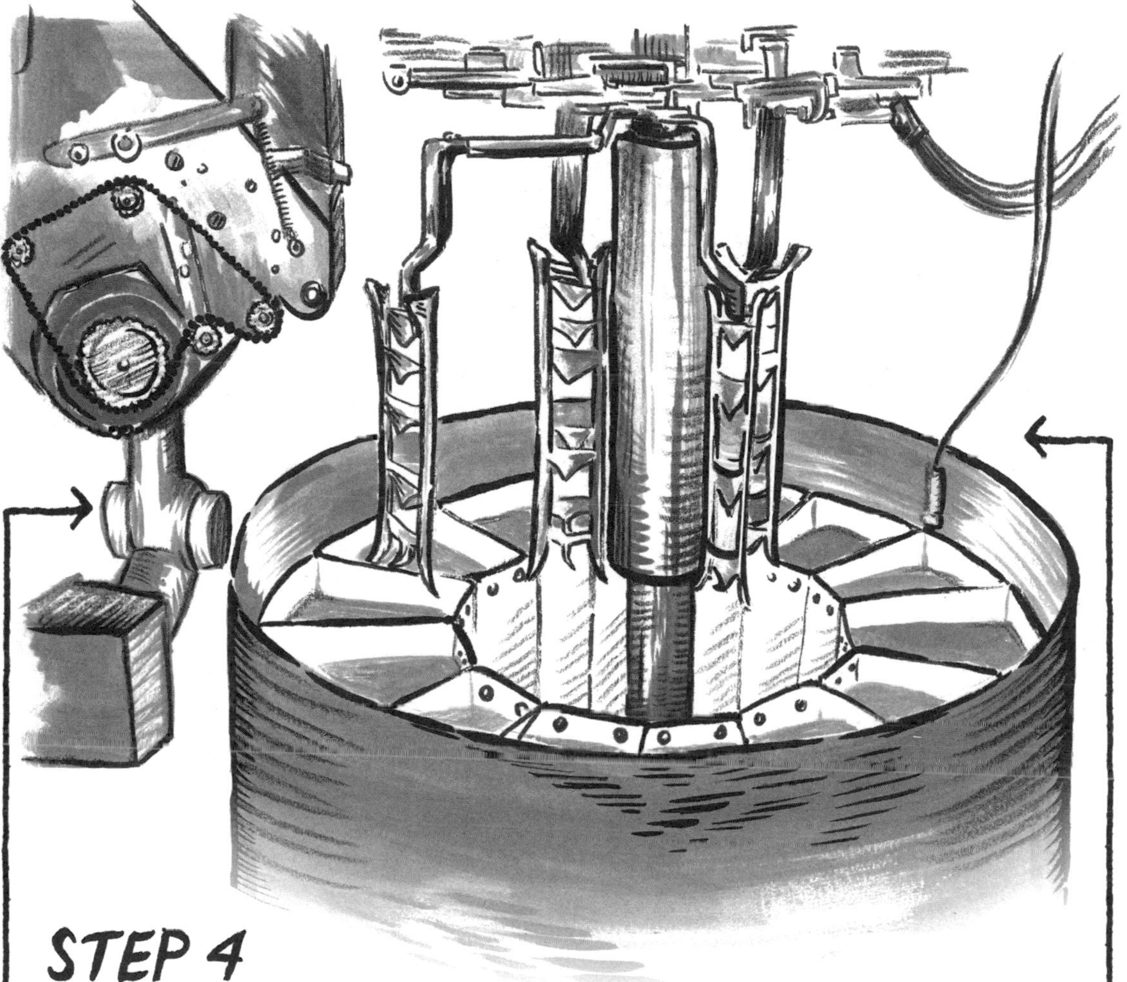

STEP 4

At the end of the cycle the arm triggers a feed which delivers the photos to a chute.

Some photobooths have blow dryers which shoot air as the photostrip is coming out.

The tanks hold photo development chemicals and water. The chemicals need to be warm enough to produce good photos, so photobooths often have thermostats and heaters.

The second most common system for a chemical photobooth is a Colour Processor or New Processor. This is the system used in Canada.

Instead of tanks, the photos slide through rollers in shallow baths. Below the baths are sealed jugs that pump the chemicals in and out.

It's a much cleaner system. However, most of the parts are made of plastic and are more prone to breaking than the metal parts of the dip'n'dunk.

Side view of camera, where the photos slide out, and fall into first set of rollers.

Most photobooths have a serial plate. A model number can give you an idea of when that booth was made and which system it uses. Though the meaning of the model number can vary from country to country.

Some models are now very rare and coveted. A Model 11 is like the Cadillac of photobooths.

Other models, like 14, 17P or 22 are still in common use in Canada and the United States.

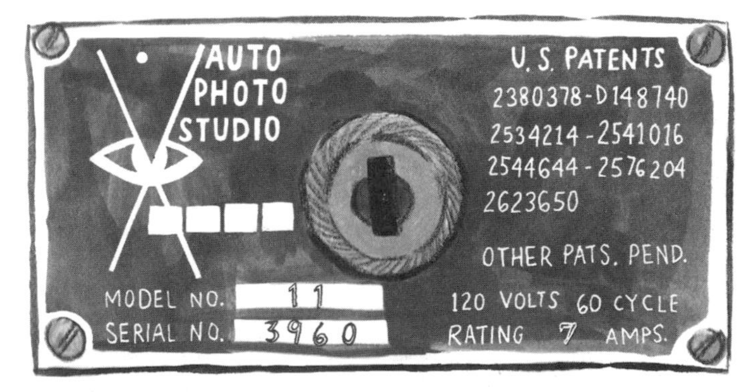

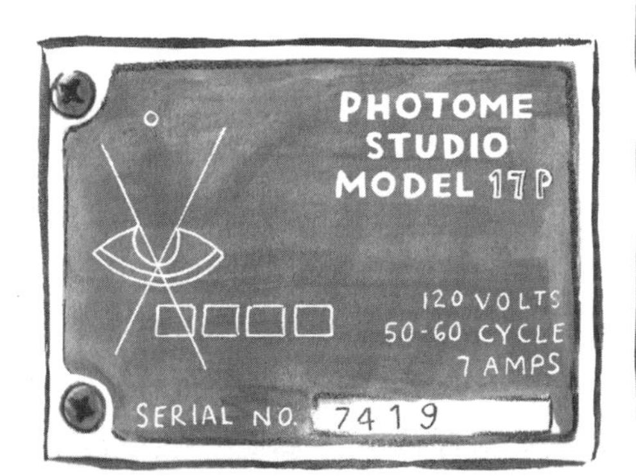

A chemical photobooth is high maintenance. It needs to be serviced once a week, needs a fresh batch of chemicals every four to six weeks and needs new film every 900 strips. All of this is quite expensive.
The introduction of digital photobooths has drastically altered the chemical photobooth industry.
PHOTOBO
3 MINUTES
3 DOLLARS
The paper for colour photos stopped being made in 2007. The stockpile is being used up and is projected to be gone by summer 2015.
Currently, there is only one supplier in the world still making the B&W paper, if they stop photobooths will disappear from public places entirely within five to ten years.
Certain darkroom chemicals are known to be hazardous, which has led the European Union to flag a chemical that photobooths require.
If the importation and manufacturing of this chemical is banned, chemical photobooths across Europe could be illegal to opeate as early as 2016.

SO, WITH ALL OF THESE FACTORS, WHY NOT SWITCH TO DIGITAL?

EDITING

Some digital booths give you the option to re-take your photos until you're happy with them. I prefer the surprise and candid nature of chemical photobooths.

QUALITY

We don't know the longevity of the ink or paper used in digital photobooths. We do know that it's easily faded by the sun and isn't used for archival purposes.

There are photos from chemical booths that are still in pristine condition, almost ninety years later.

ORIGINALITY & PRIVACY

Digital booths store copies of all the pictures they take. This is great for a booth at a party; photos can easily be shared with guests online. But what about digital booths in malls or in bars? The photobooth company owns the image files and rights, not the customer.

Each chemical photobooth picture is unique. The process doesn't produce a film negative.

LIFESPAN

Digital booths have to keep up with the latest technology, so every five to ten years they get trashed en masse. Whereas, chemical models from the 1940s are still in use today.

I'm not the only one who has a passion for vintage photobooths. And I'm not the only one who's noticed that they're disappearing.

KATE, ARTIST, ENGLAND

JEFF, ENTHUSIAST, CANADA

KATHERINE, COLLECTOR, AUSTRALIA

RUTHIE "BOOTHIE", USA

LOU, ARTIST, ENGLAND

MARCO, ARTIST, ITALY

Rather than lamenting the death of the photobooth, many people have chosen instead to form a community and champion the cause of the chemical photobooth.

IGOR, OWNER, FRANCE

VIOLETA, ARTIST, USA

They are fans, artists, collectors, technicians, and small business owners.

Photobooths have been largely overlooked in history books.

Photography surveys have dismissed them as commonplace tools and the science and innovation field view them as novelties.

They occupy a space all their own, which is somehow both incredibly mainstream and amazingly niche.

I feel it's important to tell the story of photobooths while they can still ocassionally be found and enjoyed.

By researching the past and by piecing together my own memories, I've tried to construct portraits, sometimes to celebrate and other times to commemorate, the ultimate portrait-making machines.

MILLBOURNE
MARKET MALL
EDMONTON

-Extinct-

PART I

$10 QUARTERS $10
BANK PRODUCTS, N.Y.
UNITED STATES OF AMERICA
QUARTER DOLLAR

The concept of an automatic photographic machine emerged about fifty years after the invention of photography.

1839 The invention of the first photographic processes dramatically changed the whole world. First, the French painter, Louis J.M. Daguerre announced the Daguerreotype. Shortly after, the British inventor, William Fox Talbot announced the Calotype.

The Daguerreotype

Both processes, though very different, required specific instruments and chemicals, making early photography expensive, time consuming and not very portable.

1888 The world became automated with the invention of the first vending machines. These furniture-sized devices sold individual sticks of gum and postcards at tourist destinations.

Coin-operated machines were a sensation!

1888 Photography lept out of the studio and into the hands of everyday people with Kodak's first Brownie Camera. It could take one hundred photos on celluloid film and changed how people interacted with the world.

The photobooth as we know it today has approximately seven predecessors. Some designs for photo machines were patented but never built and others became minor sensations.

1889 The *Exposition Universelle* drew millions to Paris to see the latest innovations. There, Ernest Enjalbert demonstrated his Appareil de Photographie Automalique. The user would sit still for a three to six second exposure and after five minutes would collect a framed tintype photograph.

The machines broke down regularly, were expensive and produced an image of poor quality. Enjalbert's invention was short lived but an important first step.

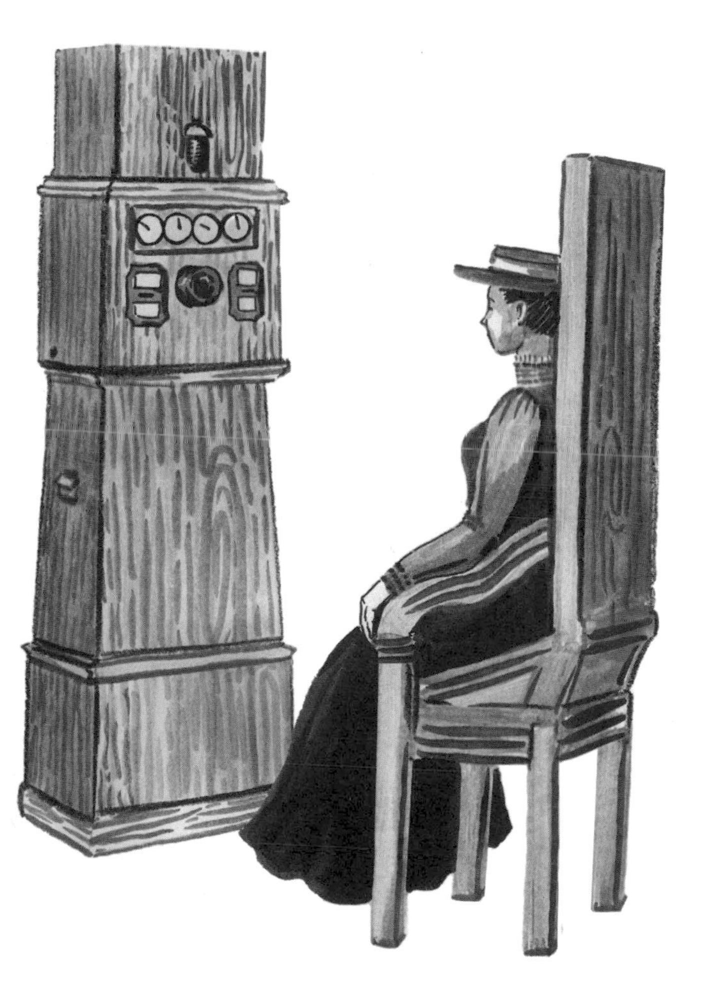

The Appareil's face plate.

1893 At an international exposition of amateur photography in Hamburg, the German inventor, Conrad Bernitt, presented the Bosco Automat.

It produced a tintype photograph in three minutes for less than Enjalbert's machine. The delicate picture was framed and came with a high-quality sleeve.

It was popular in France and used by the upper and middle classes at amusement parks and at outdoor concerts. The photographs were sensitive to oil from finger prints and to sunlight.

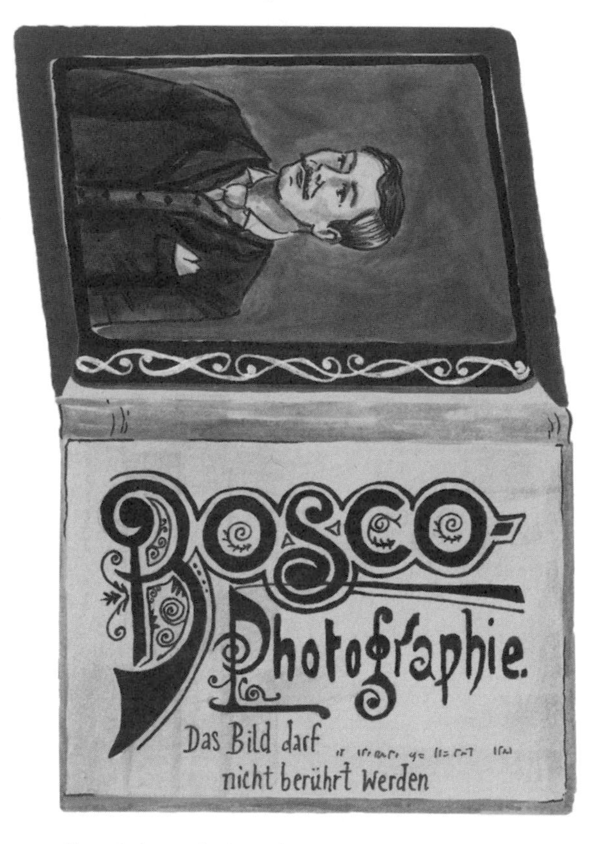

The photographs had black and gold metal frames and were protected in embossed red leather cases.

1900

Advancements in studio photography streamlined the process and reduced the cost. Penny Photos is a term for inexpensive pictures that could be taken at studios or in some arcades.

Multiple photographs could be taken on one glass negative, then printed on a sheet of paper and cut into strips. They can confusingly resemble photobooth strips but are not related.

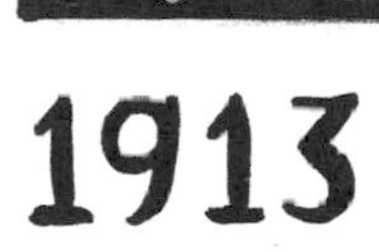

1913

A new invention, the Automatic Photographic Device, proved to be a better design.

Unlike earlier machines, it didn't require a negative or glass plate. The image went directly to paper, producing a postcard with the sitter's picture. The inventor, Ashton-Wolff made it user friendly, with a bell that rang once to prepare you for the camera, and again four minutes later when it was ready.

1915 In the United States, General Electric manufactured a coin-operated tintype machine that produced photos on small round discs. Later models of these machines were still in production into the late 20s.

1916 Spiridione Grossi, was a British inventor and owner of a photography studio. He patented a Strip Printing Photographic Apparatus. He had begun work on the apparatus in 1910 and refined the process wherein a negative moved from one end of a "traveling box" to another, exposing five or six side by side images. A second negative fixed in place produced text on each image. The device was semi-automatic but still required a human operator. The images were developed by hand.

The back side was coated with an adhesive, like postage stamps. Grossi called them Sticky Backs.

2

In the 19th Century, there were few places as isolated as Tomsk, Siberia. Yet this was the backdrop of Anatol Josephowitz's adolescence.

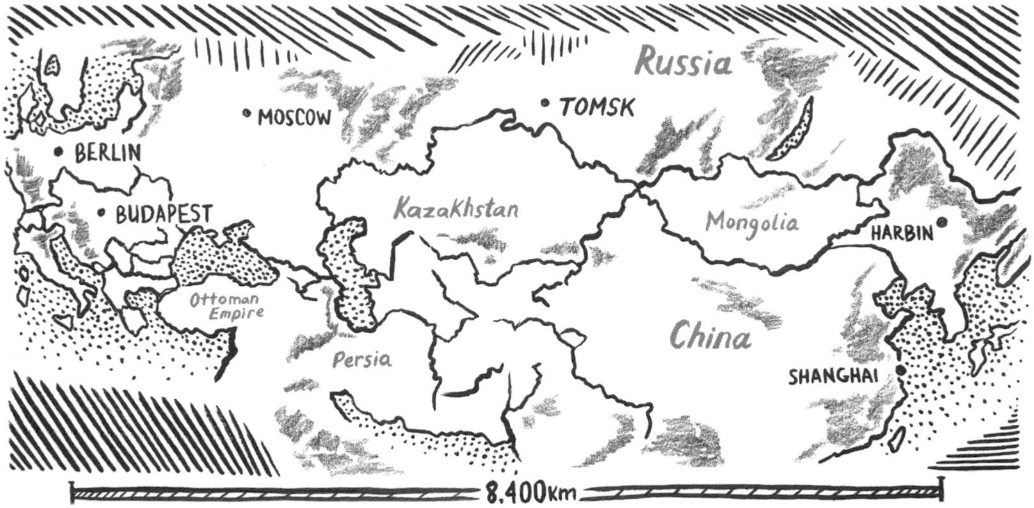

Russia
MOSCOW
TOMSK
BERLIN
BUDAPEST
Kazakhstan
Mongolia
HARBIN
Ottoman Empire
China
Persia
SHANGHAI
8.400km

By 1925 he'd be a successful businessman in New York City, but in 1894, he was the new baby of a Jewish middle class jeweler and his wife.

Anatol's mother passed away when he was only two, while in childbirth. His sister, ten years his elder, and his father raised him with care, fostering his interests.

Anatol was a smart boy, gifted at learning languages, but he spent his childhood dreaming of more than the rural town could provide.

Tomsk gradually opened up, a railroad was built near it that connected Moscow and China.

Anatol heard of the new Kodak Brownie cameras and showed interest in working in photography. His father enrolled him in a local technical institute.

The world was changing and in 1909 Berlin was a sophisticated metropolis.
Anatol charmed the owner of a photography studio into hiring and training him.
HOTEL
LOKAL

CAMERA OBSCURA
PLATEHOLDER
LEVELING STAND.
VIEWING GLASS
POWDERED ROUGE
CLAMP OF IODINE BOX
MERCURY
LIME
BROMIDE
HAND-TINTED PHOTOGRAPH
There he learned the art and science of portrait photography.

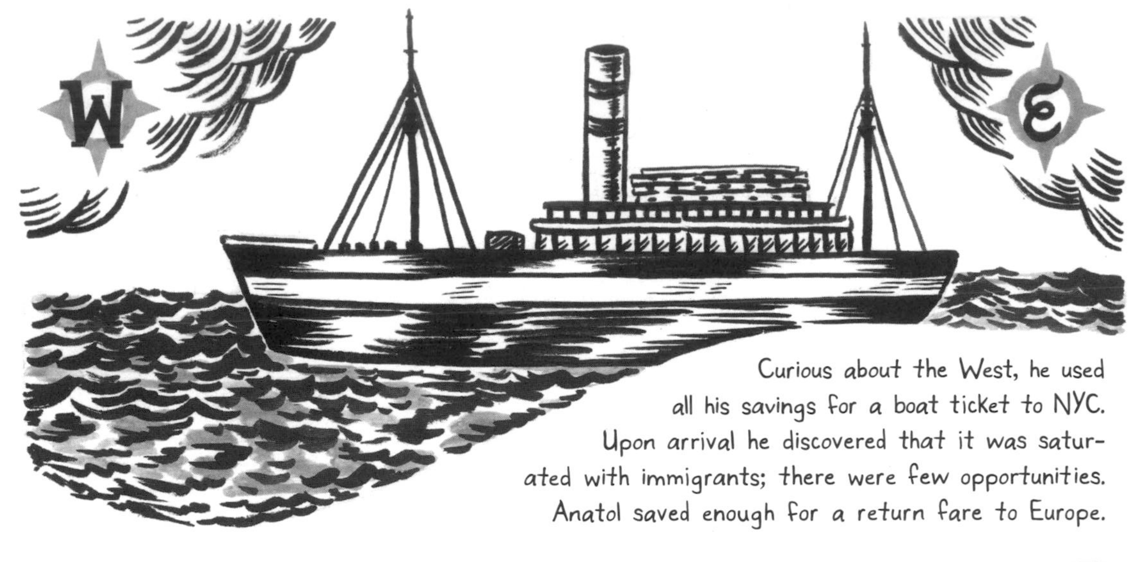

Curious about the West, he used all his savings for a boat ticket to NYC. Upon arrival he discovered that it was saturated with immigrants; there were few opportunities. Anatol saved enough for a return fare to Europe.

He arrived in Austria-Hungary and opened a studio in Budapest, which gave him the freedom to experiment with photo techniques.

He began to sketch ideas for an automatic photo making machine. In the next few years he built primitive prototypes.

His business was doing well, but in 1914, the Austro-Hungarian Empire became a tumultuous place for Russians.

The empire's Archduke, Franz Ferdinand and his wife had been assassinated.

"ALL THE NEWS, THAT'S FIT TO PRINT"

The New York Times.

THE WEATHER

VOL. LXIII ... SUNDAY, AUGUST 2, 1914 PRICE FIVE CENTS

GERMANY DECLARES WAR ON RUSSIA, FIRST SHOTS ARE FIRED; FRANCE IS MOBILIZING AND MAY BE DRAWN IN TOMORROW; PLANS TO RESCUE THE 100,000 AMERICANS NOW IN EUROPE

Austria-Hungary, Germany, the Ottoman Empire and Bulgaria declared war against Russia, France and the United Kingdom.

Kaiser signs order mobilizing his army / England hesitates

GERMANY'S WAR CHALLENGE 7:30 LAST EVENING

EMBASSY DEPARTS

Chronology of Yesterday's Fateful Events

First Shots Fired in the Russian-German War

The war ruined the economy and Anatol's business. As a Russian, he was suspected of being a spy and was under military surveillance. He lost nearly all of his customers. He had free time to work on his invention. Anatol was likely familiar with the early photographic machines, but may have never used one.

ЦАРСТВО БЪЛГАРИЯ
ПАСПОРТЪ
ROYAUME DE BULGARIE
PASSEPORT

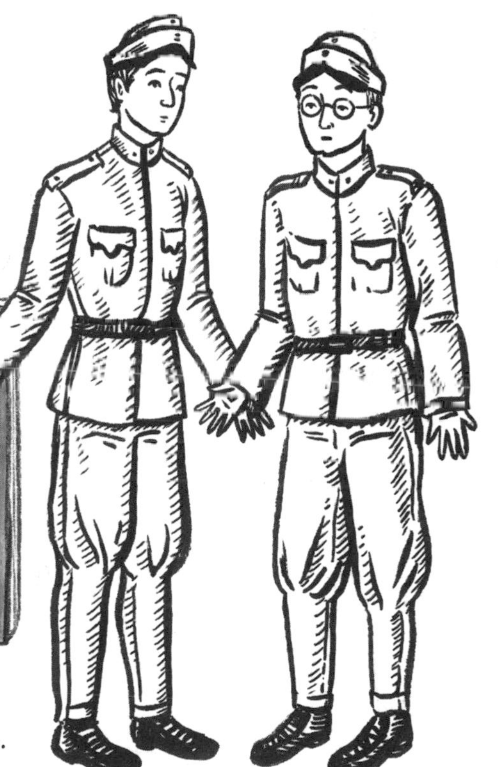

In 1919, Anatol and his friend and fellow Russian exile, E.D. Locke, fled Budapest, despite the serious dangers of traveling West to East.

They yearned to see their families in Siberia again. They got forged passports and Austrian officers' uniforms and began the 5,500 kilometre journey.

The journey was rough. The train tracks had been destroyed in many spots. They were caught in multiple conflicts and fought, escaped or bribed their way free.

Once they crossed the Russian border they quickly destroyed their uniforms but the Bolsheviks still suspected they were spies or traitors. They were imprisoned at the Siberian border with almost no food, clothing or clean water.

Anatol occupied those days by thinking of his invention. His blueprints were lost, he kept it all in his head. Eventually, the men escaped only to enter the wilderness. They had no maps, provisions or winter clothing. They traveled during the night on foot.

A thousand kilometres from home, they were imprisoned in Chelyabinsk for three weeks. Gradually Anatol, with charm and persuasion, befriended the guards and convinced them that they weren't spies...
...but just young homesick Russians. Anatol and Locke got lucky. The guards released them and gave them passage on a train.
ДА ЗДРАВСТВУЕТ
Anatol had an emotional reunion with his father but it was bittersweet.
His home had been devastated by the strains of war. Many of his old friends were dead.
The 1917 revolution caused a tense change in power and now the country was controlled by the Red Army.

By 1921, Anatol couldn't stay any longer, the USSR was officially formed months later.
He hopped trains until he arrived in Harbin, Manchuria where he sold Eastern goods to Western retailers.
With some money he continued to Shanghai. The Chinese Communist Party had just been established. The climate was mixed, with wealthy entrepreneurs and struggling locals on the same blocks.
Now 27 years old, he was determined to work in his field. He changed his last name from Josephowitz to Josepho and opened JOSEPHO STUDIOS, where he quickly established himself as a good photographer.
龙饭店
乐
JOSEPHO
影城
Anatol spent his spare time perfecting a photo process that didn't require negatives. He was ready to build the first model. After three years in China he decided to return to America, this time to seek funders.

In 1923 Anatol docked in Seattle. The economy was booming. He filed a patent for an:

AUTOMATIC CAMERA FOR TAKING TIMED SEQUENCES OF PORTRAITS

He traveled to San Francisco to network and raise funds. Then he went to Los Angeles to study motion picture cameras.

HOLLYWOODLAND

Weeks before his arrival this sign was erected to promote a new neighbourhood.

To raise money he sold an invention to Crane Plumbing for a mechanism that made it possible for a faucet lo draw hot and cold water from a single lever. Still though, he didn't have enough funds.

Anatol moved to New York City and set up a meeting with a potential investor, the owner of a printing company.

The investor brought his daughter, Ganna to the lunch.

She and Analol were instantly enamoured.

Ganna was an actress in Yiddish silent films, known for her natural charisma and poise.

Anatol and Ganna were married two weeks later. They honeymooned in Europe.

1925 With the help of Ganna's family, Anatol raised the rest of the funds he needed to manufacture delicate custom parts and for a six month lease on a good-sized studio on Broadway.

Anatol's invention, fourteen years in the making, was ready.

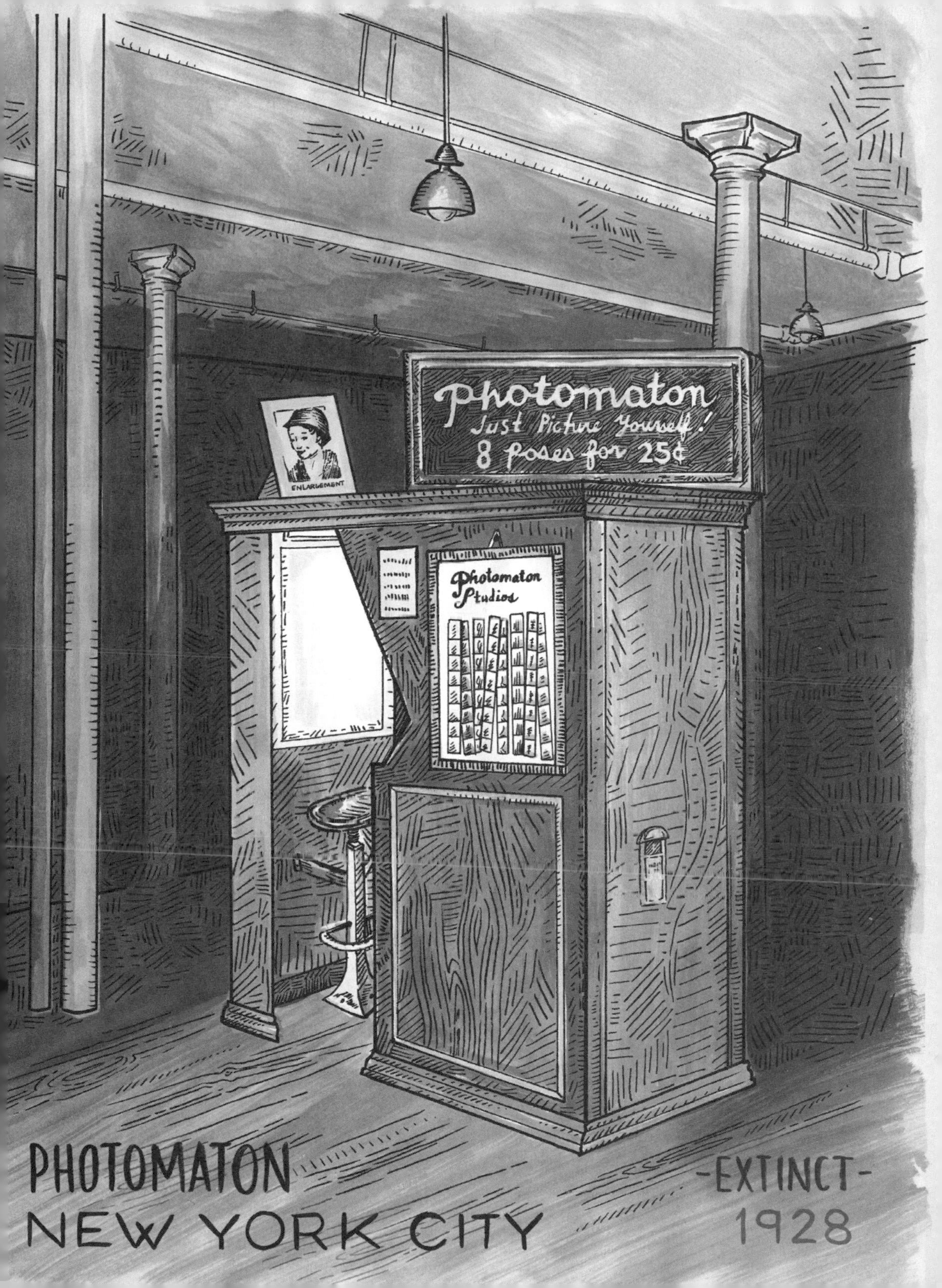
Photomaton
Just Picture Yourself!
8 poses for 25¢
ENLARGEMENT
Photomaton
Studios
PHOTOMATON
NEW YORK CITY
-EXTINCT-
1928

1997

I grew up in a big, bare and beige house. We moved there when I was six because our family had become too large for our cosy old home. There was no attic to explore, no trees to climb, no adventures to be had.

One day, when I was home without my parents, in search of something mysterious, I went to my mom's closet. I pulled out a small, old suitcase that she had forbidden me from touching. Inside, I found a journal, with a teal and gold silk cover.

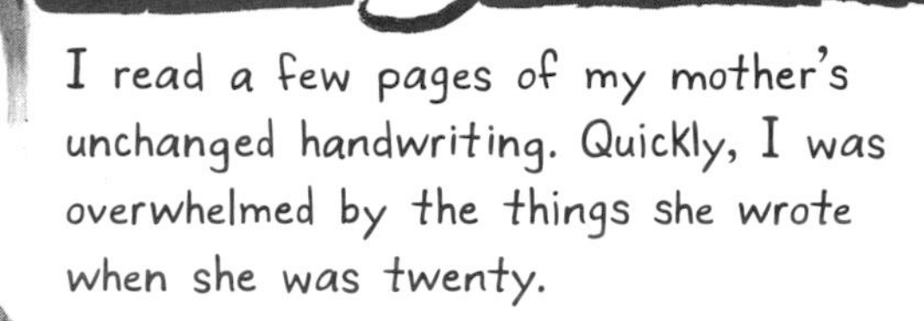

I read a few pages of my mother's unchanged handwriting. Quickly, I was overwhelmed by the things she wrote when she was twenty.

Before then, I hadn't really grasped that she was a person before I was born.

2007

In the summer, I helped my parents with a big clean-up of their house. Reminiscing, my mom pulled out the little suitcase.

It felt odd to look through it so freely. I was the same age she was in those journal entries.

We found a few photobooth pictures of her from when she was about twenty years old.

They were everyday pictures. She probably took them because she needed an I.D. photo.

I instantly felt a sense of ownership over them.

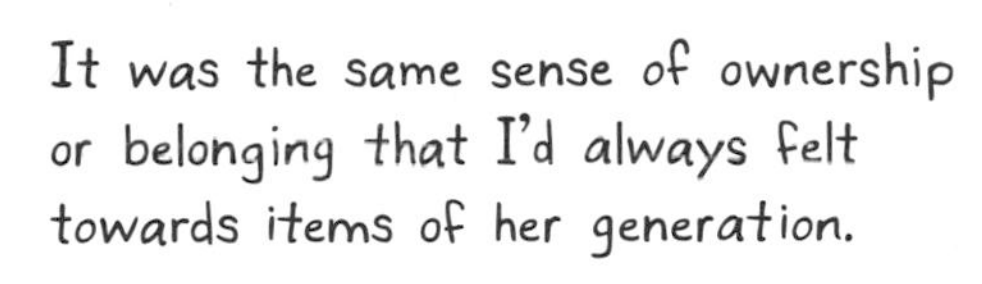

It was the same sense of ownership or belonging that I'd always felt towards items of her generation.

I turned thirteen in 2000.
I came of age in a time with big expectations, but with little to define it. My misplaced nostalgia was amplified by this uncertain decade.

Angsty and awkward, I spent most of my time in my bedroom.

Photobooths were this presence from the past, lingering into the present, when the digital age had already presented itself in all its glitchy glory.

>>>>>>>>> **MONDAY** **TUESDAY** **WEDNESDAY**

They were straightforward.

The sequence: money-in, photos-out, was *so* satisfying. I got an adrenaline rush each time.

A habit quickly formed.

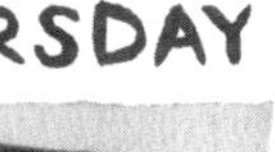

>>>>>>>>>

Taking pictures became a personal ritual.

I spent my tiny income on them. The process felt high stakes, I couldn't afford to take them over again.

It felt epic every time.

The photobooth serves as an intergenerational time machine, connecting kin through a shared activity. Each photo acts as its own time capsule.

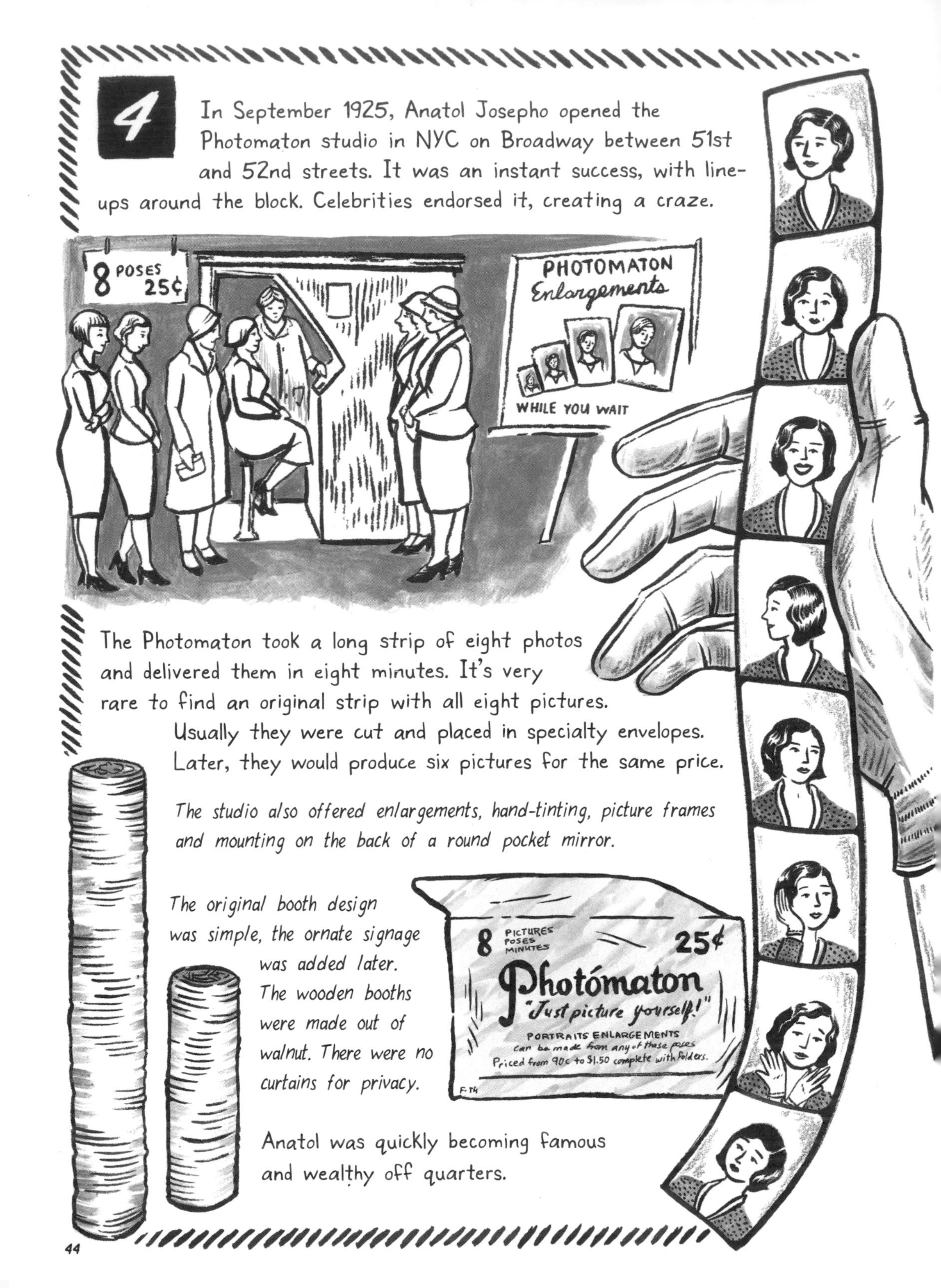
4
In September 1925, Anatol Josepho opened the Photomaton studio in NYC on Broadway between 51st and 52nd streets. It was an instant success, with line-ups around the block. Celebrities endorsed it, creating a craze.
8 POSES 25¢
PHOTOMATON Enlargements
WHILE YOU WAIT
The Photomaton took a long strip of eight photos and delivered them in eight minutes. It's very rare to find an original strip with all eight pictures.
Usually they were cut and placed in specialty envelopes. Later, they would produce six pictures for the same price.
The studio also offered enlargements, hand-tinting, picture frames and mounting on the back of a round pocket mirror.
The original booth design was simple, the ornate signage was added later. The wooden booths were made out of walnut. There were no curtains for privacy.
8 PICTURES POSES MINUTES
25¢
Photómaton
"Just picture yourself!"
PORTRAITS ENLARGEMENTS
can be made from any of these poses
Priced from 90¢ to $1.50 complete with Folders.
F-14
Anatol was quickly becoming famous and wealthy off quarters.

Time Magazine estimated that in its first six months, the Photomaton studio had over 280,000 customers.

The studio expanded to meet demand and in 1926 a Photomaton factory opened. Soon Anatol was overseeing the production of many more machines.

The Photomaton wasn't just new trendy technology, it was a cultural phenomenon, a marker of a new era.

Taken in NYC in 1926. ⟶
The photos were narrower and slightly smaller than the photobooth pictures today.

Like a time machine, the Photomaton suspended the sitter in space before propelling them into the future.

1927 Henry Morgenthau Sr. assembled a team of investors and offered Anatol $1,000,000 for the rights to his company. Anatol accepted and was made the Vice President.

← *Anatol and Henry*

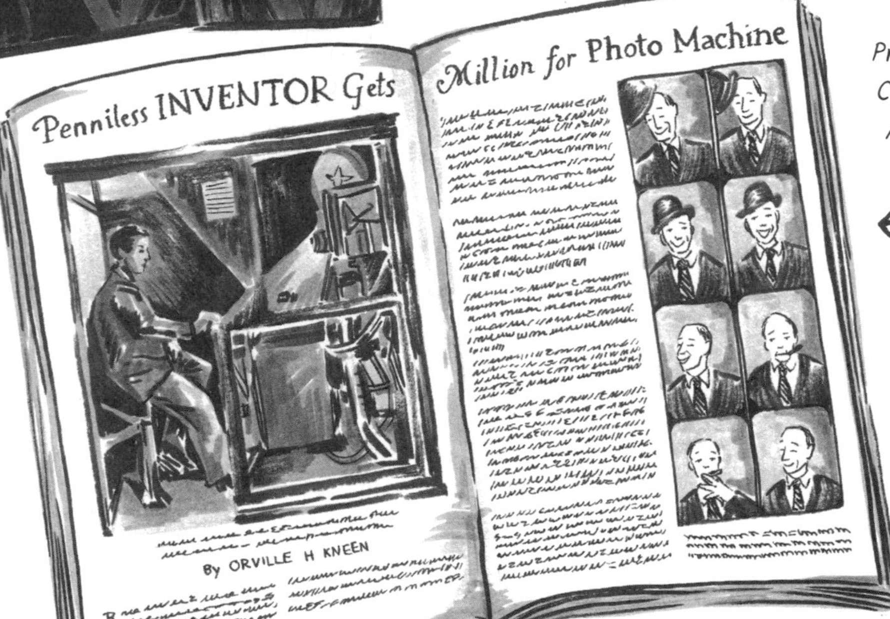

Presidential Candidate Al Smith ↵

HENRY MORGENTHAU SR. →

- *American Ambassador to the Ottoman Empire during WWI*
- *Co-founder of the Red Cross*
- *Director of Underwood Typewriter Company*
- *Has the same birthday as me, April 26*

Franklin D. Roosevelt was appointed one of the directors of the consortium, before he became President of the United States in 1933. They installed 220 Photomatons across the country by 1928. These studios varied from tented areas on boardwalks to marble showrooms.

Investors bought the rights from Anatol for England, France, Germany, Italy and Canada, forming the British Photomaton Parent Corporation and the Société Continentale Photomaton.

Paper stock share from the publicly traded French company.

The highly anticipated opening of Photomaton Studio in Potsdamer Platz, Berlin, in 1929.

In the wake of his success, Anatol donated $500,000 to various charities and started a fund for inventors in need of financial aid.
In 1928, Ganna and Anatol became parents to a baby boy, Marco, named after Anatol's father. A couple years later they had another son, Roy.
His became known as the ultimate rags to riches story and he was the poster boy for the hardworking immigrant. The American press loved his story.
STRAND
ARTIE SHAW
Photomaton
8 PORTRAITS 25¢
La Regina
STRAND
The photobooth didn't begin and end with Anatol's design. Many others made improvements and patented their variations. John Slack worked for The Photomaton Company and made these improvements:
• refined the paper delivery unit for fewer jams
• made the "plumbless" machine so it didn't need to be attached to a water source
• sped up the development from eight to four minutes
• made a gauge to control the temperature in the booth
• thought of mirrored glass so the poser could see their reflection

At the same time, profiteering individuals attempted to design similar machines and set up competition on Broadway. One of these companies, Photomovette, was sued by The Photomaton Co. for patent infringement and for nearly stealing their slogan.

Some companies accepted special tokens instead of quarters because fake quarters or "slugs" were a problem.

Some early competitors, who weren't able to design a fully automated photo machine, would make it appear like they had by hiring a person to hide inside and develop the pictures by hand.

One story recounts an exploitative company, likely run by the mafia, that employed little people to develop pictures in the dark, poorly ventilated, hot booths at carnivals and fairs.

"Photomaton Girl" at a fair in the United States.

The Photomaton studios had attendants to give instructions, upsell customers on enlargements and sometimes to take the money and push a button to trigger the camera. Though the machines were fully automated, customer service was still expected as part of the experience.

The role women may have played in the history and success of the photobooth has not been documented. These attendants were the female presence in the otherwise male-dominated industry.

"Miss Photomaton" in a department store in France.

ATTENDANT, EXHIBITION

THE Services of Smart Young Girl are required for Photomatic Machine at Exhibition. Telephone 43-550 for appointment.

Ad for another company in New Zealand newspaper.

Photomaton FRANCE EXTINCT

5

My reputation as "the photobooth girl" was solidified by 2004. Unlike the official Photomaton Girls of decades earlier, no one trained me how to best use a photobooth. The process was more intuitive than it was formulaic.

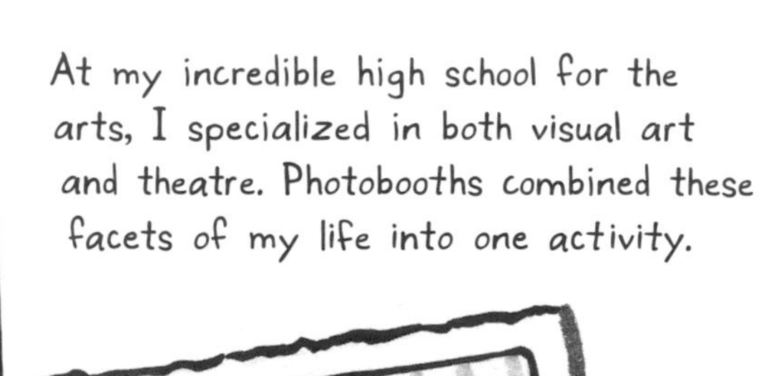

At my incredible high school for the arts, I specialized in both visual art and theatre. Photobooths combined these facets of my life into one activity.

Each time I used one, it felt like a performance. But more accurately, all those after school visits were rehearsals. I was refining my skills.

Photobooths became my personal theatres, conveniently located all around the city for me to use as creative retreats.

I was both the performer and the audience.

The colourless frame created context for the image, defining the space where the subject lives and setting the boundary of the booth's conditions.

The white borders are to the photobooth what red velvet curtains are to the stage.

In the ninth grade, as a shy fourteen year old, I somehow made it on the improv team. It took me a year to come out of my shell and once I did, I got pretty good at it.
The skills I learned on the improv team: thinking on my feet, following my impulses, considering stage pictures, and playing characters, all carried over into the booth.
Posing for pictures is a skill. Timing, composition and lighting are things you learn by trial and error.
Experimenting with a mirror and tinfoil as the background.
My very awkward attempt at artful nudes.
When I was sixteen I was scouted at an improv competition and joined the professional company in Edmonton. I started doing weekly shows in front of large audiences and I kept it up for many years, with various companies, in cities all over.

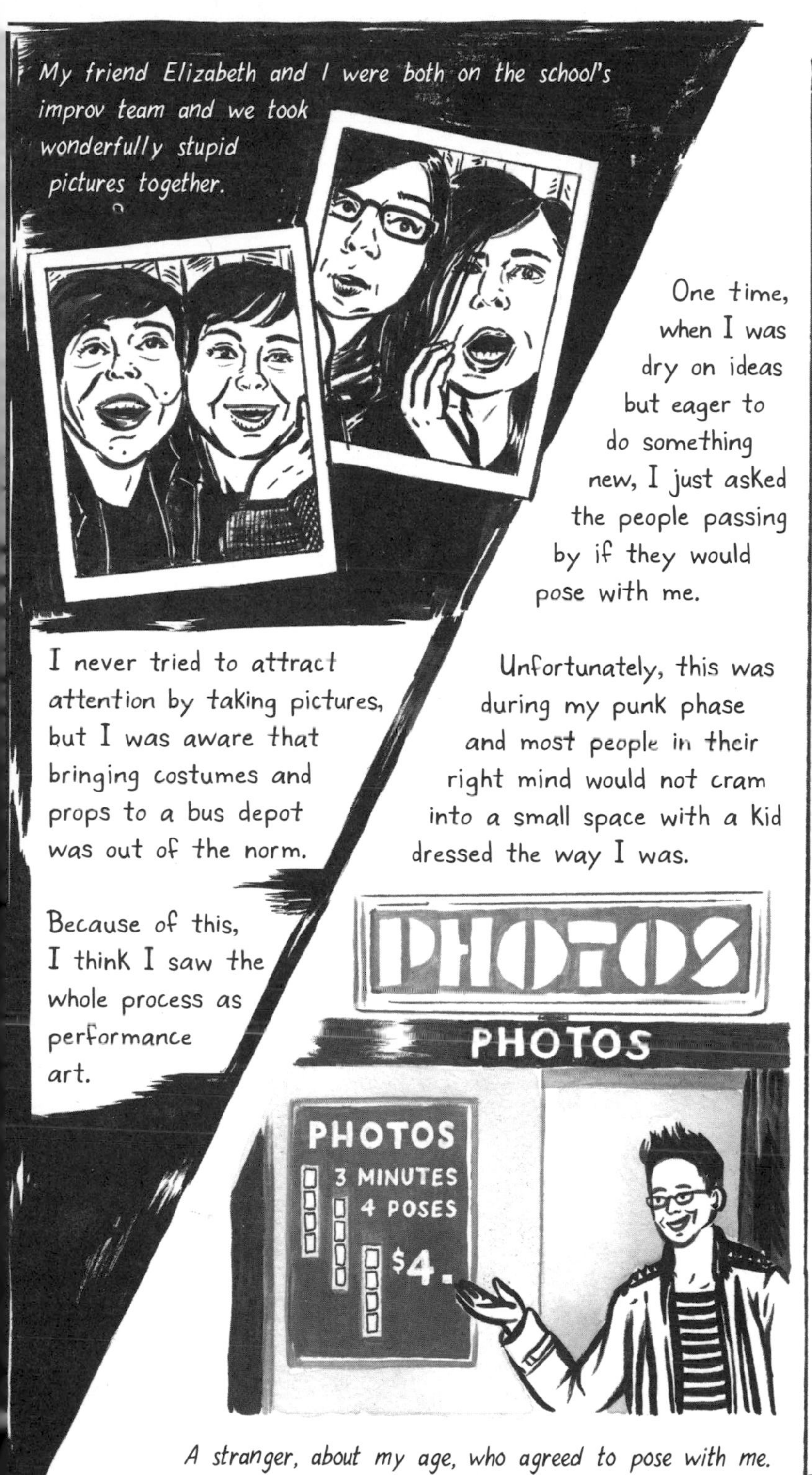

A stranger, about my age, who agreed to pose with me. She didn't wait to see how the photos turned out.

Russian immigrant and machinist, William Rabkin, bought the fledging International Mutoscope Reel Company in the mid-20s. They produced hand-cranked motion picture viewers. Rabkin set out to save the company by designing an improved photographic machine.

Modern Mechanix Magazine, Nov. 1936

New Automatic Machine Delivers Metal-Framed Photos

Left - The "Photomatic" delivers metal-framed photos. Right - Its mechanism.

IN LESS than one minute, a new coin-operated machine snaps a photo of the operator, develops it, and delivers the finished photo encased in a metal frame. The operator has only to sit down, look into a mirror to assure the desired pose, and insert a coin. The novel machine does the rest.

The photo produced by the machine, framed is 2⅝ x 3⅛ inches in size. The back of the photo has a lined space on which the date and place where the photo was taken can be inscribed. A special duplicator device incorporated in the machine makes it possible to secure additional metal-framed copies of any photo taken by the machine.

The "Photomatic," as the machine is called, is housed in a cabinet occupying floor space of about 2½ x 4 feet. It is 73 inches in height. The operating unit is mounted on the door of the cabinet for quick and easy inspection.

In 1934 the International Mutoscope Reel Company launched the *PHOTOMATIC*. It was half the size of the Photomaton and had an art deco exterior. It was made out of automobile steel and painted in bright enamel colours.

Internally, the system operated very differently from the Photomaton. It was more efficient, with only a 50 second wait for the photo. The whole thing weighed only 600 pounds and was built in four parts for easy shipping and assembly.

The photos cost anywhere between $0.10 and $0.25, which would be $1.75 to $4.25 today.

The Deluxe Photomatic was made in the early 40s. The sitter adjusted her/his height in the photo by turning a knob which raised or lowered the camera, rather than turning the stool up or down.

Photomatic
TRADE MARK
DIRECTIONS
DO NOT INSERT COIN WHILE RED LIGHT IS ON
1. ADJUST SEAT TO PROPER HEIGHT, SO THAT YOUR EYES ARE ON LEVEL WITH LINE ON MIRROR.
2. SIT SLIGHTLY SIDEWAYS AND LOOK INTO MIRROR OR LENS.
3. INSERT COIN; MAKE SURE NOT TO MOVE WHILE LARGE LIGHTS ARE ON.
4. WHEN LARGE LIGHTS GO OUT, LEAVE BOOTH AND WAIT FOR PICTURE TO DROP INTO CHUTE AT RIGHT.
MACHINE NO. DP220
MADE IN USA BY
INTERNATIONAL MUTOSCOPE REEL CO. INC
NEW YORK CITY

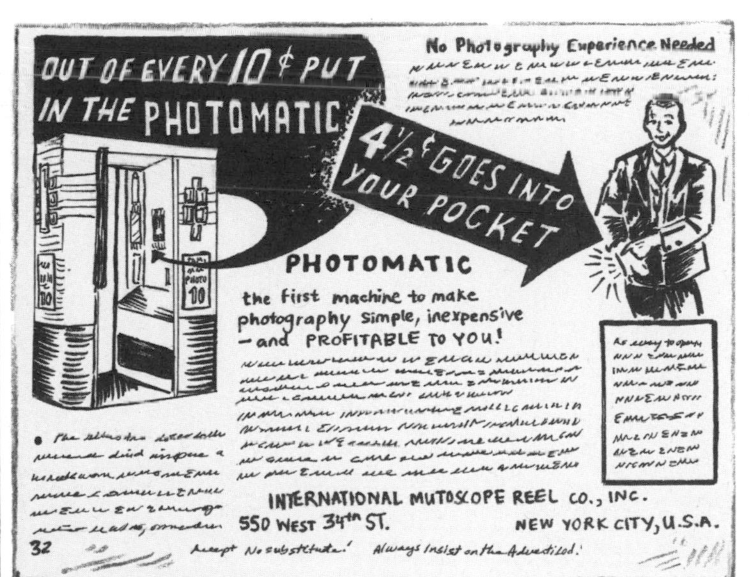

Businesses interested in buying a Photomatic could get it in any colour scheme and could choose from various models. The average yearly gross for a single Photomatic was $5,200 in today's dollars.

Unlike the Photomaton, the Photomatic produced a single photo, already framed in metal, cardboard or plastic. It depended on the materials available during WWII.

The actual photo quality of Photomatics was mediocre, but the framing and photo-taking experience was so great that it didn't matter to customers.

Today they are the most highly valued photobooth pictures by collectors, the coloured metal frames being the most desirable.

Photomatic pictures from my collection, with a cardboard frame and metal frame.

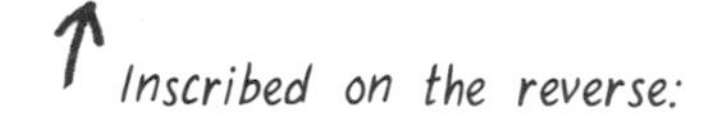

Inscribed on the reverse:

DATE *April 1* **TAKEN** *Hotel St.*
MESSAGE *Wishes, luck & all that! Jeanne*

My maternal grandfather, Alphonse. Photo was removed from its frame, presumably so it could be carried in a wallet.

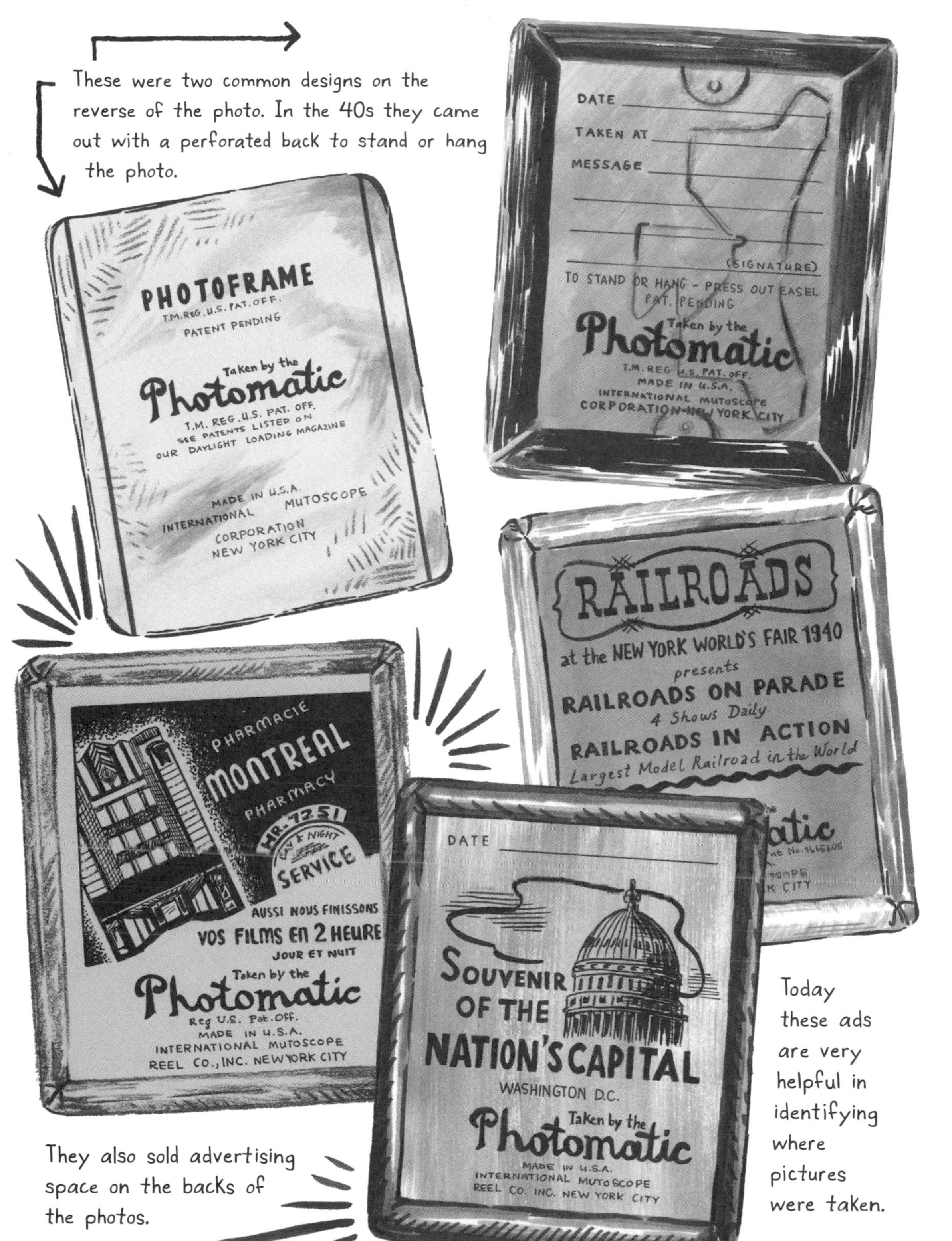
These were two common designs on the reverse of the photo. In the 40s they came out with a perforated back to stand or hang the photo.
PHOTOFRAME
T.M. REG. U.S. PAT. OFF.
PATENT PENDING
Taken by the
Photomatic
T.M. REG. U.S. PAT. OFF.
SEE PATENTS LISTED ON
OUR DAYLIGHT LOADING MAGAZINE
MADE IN U.S.A.
INTERNATIONAL MUTOSCOPE
CORPORATION
NEW YORK CITY
DATE
TAKEN AT
MESSAGE
(SIGNATURE)
TO STAND OR HANG - PRESS OUT EASEL
PAT. PENDING
Taken by the
Photomatic
T.M. REG. U.S. PAT. OFF.
MADE IN U.S.A.
INTERNATIONAL MUTOSCOPE
CORPORATION NEW YORK CITY
RAILROADS
at the NEW YORK WORLD'S FAIR 1940
presents
RAILROADS ON PARADE
4 Shows Daily
RAILROADS IN ACTION
Largest Model Railroad in the World
PHARMACIE
MONTREAL
PHARMACY
HR. 7251
DAY & NIGHT
SERVICE
AUSSI NOUS FINISSONS
VOS FILMS EN 2 HEURE
JOUR ET NUIT
Taken by the
Photomatic
Reg U.S. Pat. Off.
MADE IN U.S.A.
INTERNATIONAL MUTOSCOPE
REEL CO., INC. NEW YORK CITY
DATE
SOUVENIR
OF THE
NATION'S CAPITAL
WASHINGTON D.C.
Taken by the
Photomatic
MADE IN U.S.A.
INTERNATIONAL MUTOSCOPE
REEL CO. INC. NEW YORK CITY
They also sold advertising space on the backs of the photos.
Today these ads are very helpful in identifying where pictures were taken.

TODAY'S PICTURE TOMORROW'S TREASURE

The Int. Mutoscope Reel Company and their holding company, the National Photomatic Corporation had the exclusive rights to photobooths in these locations:

- NEW YORK'S SUBWAY SYSTEM
- STATEN ISLAND FERRY TERMINAL
- NEW YORK PORT AUTHORITY
- NEW YORK'S 1939 WORLD FAIR
- PENN STATION
- GRAND CENTRAL STATION

The average person passed a couple Photomatics a day, they were even placed in public washrooms. By 1944, they were on every continent except Antarctica.

In the 50s, the company launched the Photomat, which produced unframed photos in multiples and in varying sizes. These machines often had dispensers attached to the exterior that sold protective envelopes separately.

PHOTOMATIC 1940s

Grand Central Station NYC

7

2003

One Sunday afternoon, I was walking towards a bus stop when I crossed paths with a group of teenagers that I didn't know.

I didn't normally carry a purse but I had just seen a play and was a little dressed up.

My first, foolish instinct was to reason with them. They responded by shoving me, face first into the bus shelter.

F*CK, I THINK MY NOSE IS BROKEN

I was outnumbered and knew I shouldn't try to fight back.

Eventually an elderly man at the bus stop threatened to call the police.

I was crumpled on the ground, with my hands over my face. I didn't actually see them run off.

I took the next bus home, bloody and shaken.

But I still had my purse, I still had my collection.

Soon after that, I stopped carrying my collection around with me in my wallet.

It got too big and obviously it wasn't safe anymore.

For a brief while I still kept it in my backpack, in a special pouch I had sewn just for my collection.

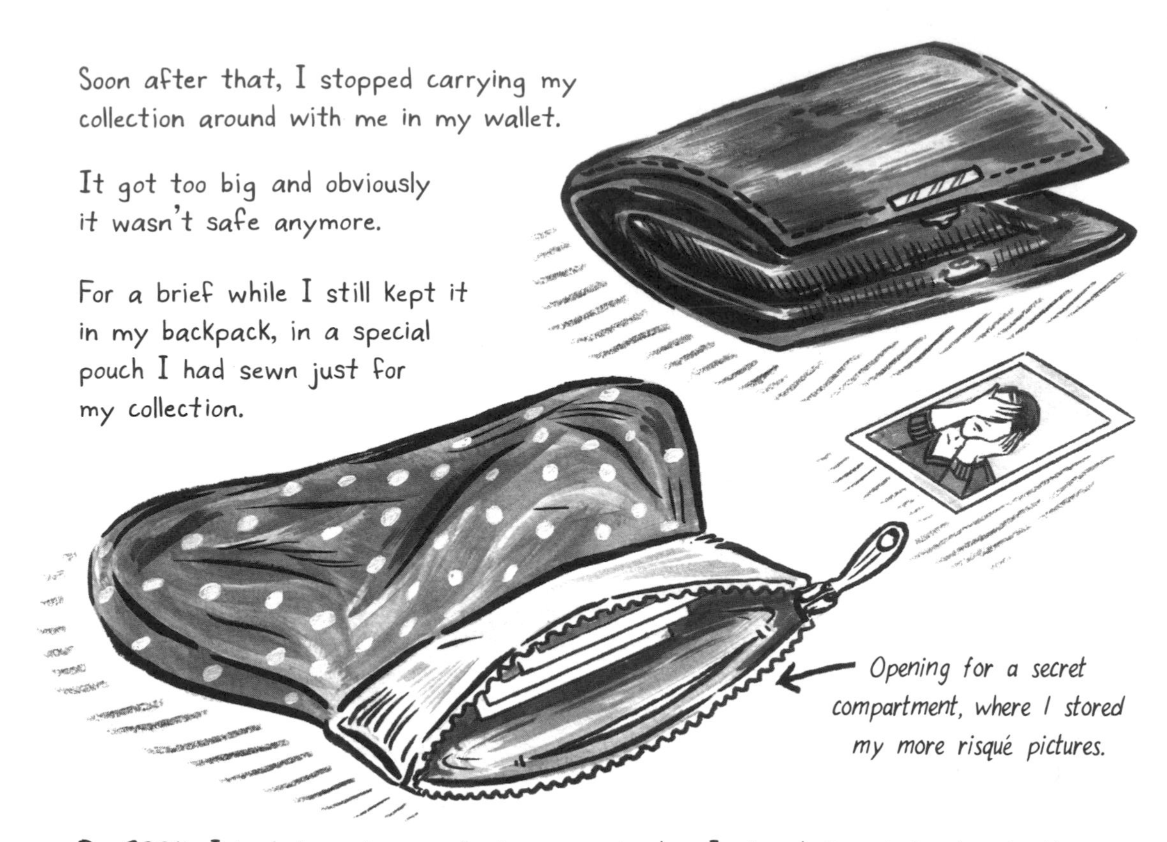

By 2004, I had to put my collection in a binder. I placed the photos in plastic sheets that are actually designed for business cards. From then on, I took colour photocopies of my photos and glued those into my sketchbook so I could still show them to my friends.

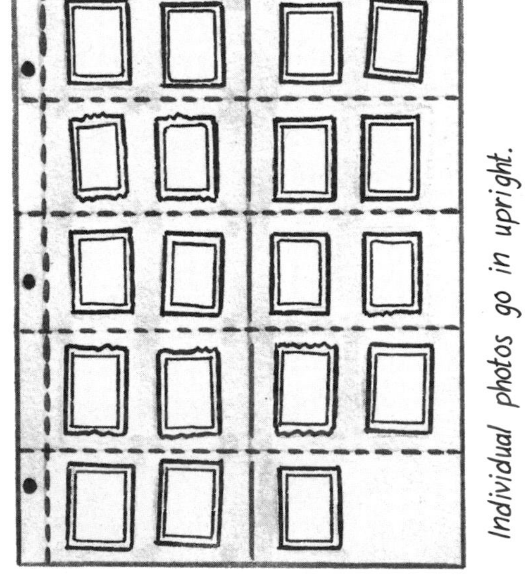

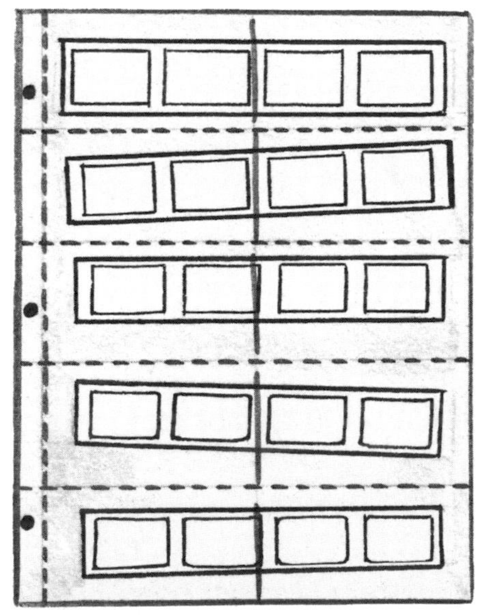

One of the photos that was in my wallet that day is actually the oldest in my collection. It's of myself, my mom and my two older sisters. I was ten and we had just seen *Spice World* in the cheap theatres. (It had been my turn to pick the movie.)

8

Anatol had conceived of and designed the Photomaton as a luxury item, but the impact it made on society is beyond measure. In 1929, the Great Depression hit, people couldn't afford studio photography, but many could still afford a quarter for a photobooth.

The variety of photobooths on the market by the 1930s, offered accessible and affordable portrait photography to all classes of people.

Decades before the Civil Rights movement, photobooths didn't discriminate against their sitters. Photobooths around the United States captured African American communities.
Photobooths allowed people to document themselves as they wanted to be seen and as they saw themselves.

The reverse side of a photobooth picture can be just as revealing and as intimate as the image.

New companies tried to distinguish themselves from the Photomaton. Scenic backgrounds became very popular.

Some machines produced larger format pictures, two or three times the size of the Photomaton's pictures.

Full-length booths were designed and set up in small studios or in trailers that would travel to fairs and rodeos.

The curtain, which became a staple of photobooths after the Photomaton, cut the sitter off from the outside world. The privacy created a safe space for gay couples to capture their relationships.

My great uncle, James Fitzgerald, during his military training in Quebec.

The Allies weren't the only ones making mementos. The global success of photobooths documented the Axis' side of the war as well.

German solider who had been awarded ribbons.

Despite the strain that WWII put on the resources that photobooths needed to operate, pictures were taken at an industry high.

During the economic boom of the 1950s, photobooth companies performed less well than expected. Their financial success was inversely correlated with the strength of the economy.

I also suspect that after the war, when people realized they would live to see another day, memento-making was less essential to their day to day lives.

Generally though, like today, most old photobooth pictures appear casual and spontaneous.

"People look different in different eras and there's no moving them backward or forward in time. Faces reflect the world they've been looking at."

— PETER EGAN

2 LARGE PHOTOS
2 SENSATIONAL! Studio-like PHOTOS 50 SECONDS
AUTOMATIC • PRIVATE
ATOMIC BOMBER
25¢
NEW! PHOTO FOLDER 10¢
2
Only 50 Seconds
25¢
PHOTOMAT
1950s -EXTINCT-

9

After high school, I moved to Calgary to do a four year degree in visual art. The environment was stimulating.

When the assignments were self-directed, I tried incorporating photobooth pictures into my larger art pieces.

But photobooth pictures weren't recognized by the art institution. My professors discouraged me from pursuing them as serious art. They were pedestrian and didn't have a place in the fine art world.
ART SCHOOL FRENZY
STUDIO TIME
CRITIQUES
LECTURES
"Photography's imprint of reality and its mechanical process of creation was considered incompatible with creative activity... photobooth artists at times get a less than serious reception, solely due to their choice of medium."
— BIRNA KLEIVAN
I demoted my interest in photobooths from art to hobby.
I wasn't aware that others were making art with photobooth pictures.

2006

To be fair to my professors, my photobooth art wasn't groundbreaking.

My ideas were one-offs. When I attempted larger, more complex pieces, my concepts weren't fully formed.

While still perserving the strip format, I started manipulating the pictures. I cut up and rearranged them, collaged them with vintage paper, burnt and melted them and even embroidered into them.

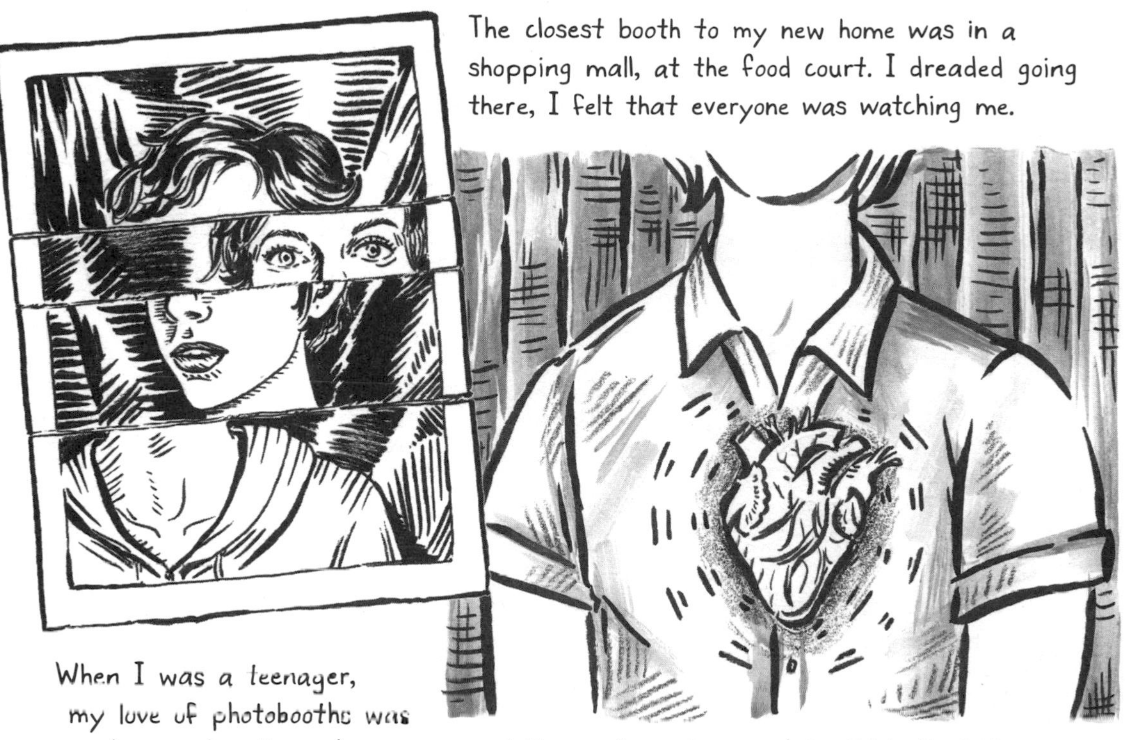
The closest booth to my new home was in a shopping mall, at the food court. I dreaded going there, I felt that everyone was watching me.
When I was a teenager, my love of photobooths was endearing to others. As a young adult, people just seemed to think that it was a weird hobby. My "photobooth girl" title seemed immature.

PHOTOS
Most of all, I hated waiting for my pictures to develop. I was embarrassed to be seen there.

10
1926
David McCowan was a Canadian inventor from rural Ontario, known for his stutter, quiet demeanor and good business sense.
In his early twenties, he created a toy company for which he designed wind-up and simple mechanical toys.
On a trip to NYC, he saw the Photomaton and was inspired to design his own photographic machine. He set to work on developing an entirely different mechanical process.
David had no background in photography so he spent long days at the nearest library, learning the science.
PHOTOGRAPHIC TECHNIQUES
ADVANCED MECHANICS
A CHEMICAL GUIDE
DARKROOM MANUAL
PHOTO CHEMISTRY
cameras & lenses
AUTOMATION
By 1927, his invention was ready. David invested $25,000 ($270,000 in today's money) on developing that first model.

The Phototeria was born.

Like the Photomaton, the Phototeria's cabin was solid wood, but the booth was much smaller. The Phototeria had wooden doors on both sides that slid shut to give the sitter complete privacy.

Inside it was whimsical, complete with a cuckoo bird that popped out to let the sitter know the camera was ready.

The Phototeria produced a photo on the back of a metal-rimmed pocket mirror in only one minute. It could develop multiple images at once, increasing the profitability.

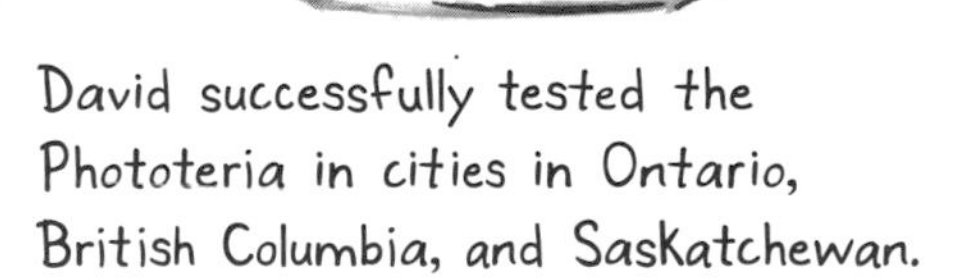

David successfully tested the Phototeria in cities in Ontario, British Columbia, and Saskatchewan.

In 1928 David brought the Phototeria to a trade show in Chicago, to sell the American and South American rights to interested buyers. Before he did any business, he was greeted by two forceful men who invited him to a hotel room.

THERE, HE WAS MET BY AL CAPONE.

I RUN THE VENDING IN THIS COUNTRY

David cancelled his meetings, packed up his Phototeria and immediately drove home.

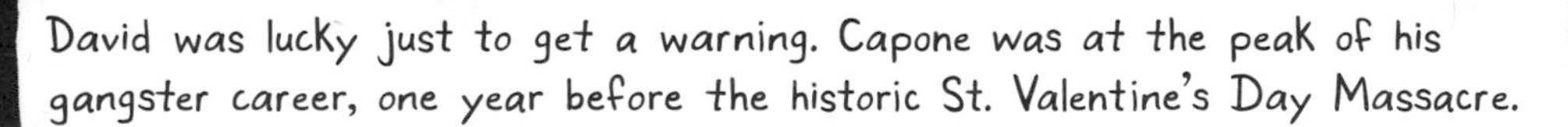

HERALD CHICAGO EXAMINER

METROPOLITAN EDITION

PRICE 5¢

15 FEBRUARY 1929

TELEPHONE

Today

FIRING SQUAD KILLS SEVEN IN BIG GANGLAND MASSACRE

At the End of Gangland's Trail!

BRITAIN MAPS OWN ARMS PLAN FOR U.S. APPROVAL

LINE UP! EXECUTIONER SNAPS; MACHINE GUNS WIPE OUT N. SIDE MOB

This was the prohibition era, Mafia families had wealth and clout. Through threats and violence, gangsters extorted money from legitimate but small vending machine companies. They also needed venues to clean their dirty money. The photobooths some "operated" weren't businesses but covers.

Gangsters Accused Of Trying to Control Vending Machines

WASHINGTON — Gangsters and racketeers were accused by Sen. John I. McClellan (D-Ark) today of seeking to take over legitimate business to the multibillion-dollar coin-operated machine industry.

Opening an investigation by his Labor-Management Committee into that industry, McClellan said underworld figures from widely scattered areas in the nation will be called as witnesses.

"The current investigation," he said, "will likely be one of the most important we have undertaken with reference to the hoodlum effort in achieve legitimacy through association with unions and business enterprise."

This practice was already established with juke boxes, laundry mats, slot machines, arcades and other machines that accepted coins.

In 1930, David sold the American rights to the National Automatic Machine Company and it was rebranded and redesigned as the Photette.

Photette

It was modernized, the wood became metal and the sliding doors became floor length curtains.

← *Coin plate from the Phototeria*

Photette's continued to produce photos on mirrors but later also produced paper photos with special designs. The machines produced borders (not frames) by using a custom stencil in the camera box that exposed and blocked light on the photo's edges.

BOARDWALK
-McCOWAN-
PHOTOTERIA
PHOTOS FRAMED 3 MINUTES
PHOTO ON MIRROR DISC
NEWEST PULP MAGAZINES
SOLD HERE
DARK
ACTION
PLANET
CRIME
MYSTERY
TRUE LOVE
AMAZING TRUE TALES
CRIME
PHOTOTERIA Extinct

The French poet, André Breton penned the Surrealist Manifesto in Paris and propelled this cultural movement forward.

1924

"Psychic automatism in its pure state, by which one proposes to express -- verbally, by means of the written word, or in any other manner -- the actual functioning of thought. Dictated by the thought, in the absence of any control exercised by reason, exempt from any aesthetic or moral concern."

Salvador Dali and his muse, Gala.

French painter, Yves Tanguy.

Friend of the Surrealists, Marie Berthe Aurenche.

The automatic, pictorial and candid nature of photobooths appealed to the Surrealists immensely. It was an instant art-making machine to them.

2008

Studying on exchange in Toronto, I took an Art History course on Dadaism and Surrealism and was captivated by the movements.

I hadn't known that the Surrealists used photobooths in their art practices, and I wouldn't know for some time, because no photobooths were mentioned in the class or textbook! The Surrealists had blurred the lines between art, life and play. Historians had overlooked the photobooth while distinguishing between these elements.

My friend, Elizabeth and I in New York City.

False mustache in Calgary.

Frame from an animation I shot in Toronto.

I think if I had been exposed to reveered photobooth art in that course, it would have probably changed how I viewed my own relationship to them.

This piece, published in the magazine *La Revolution Surrealist* in 1929, features photo-booth portraits of the 16 members of the movement, surrounding a painting by Magritte.

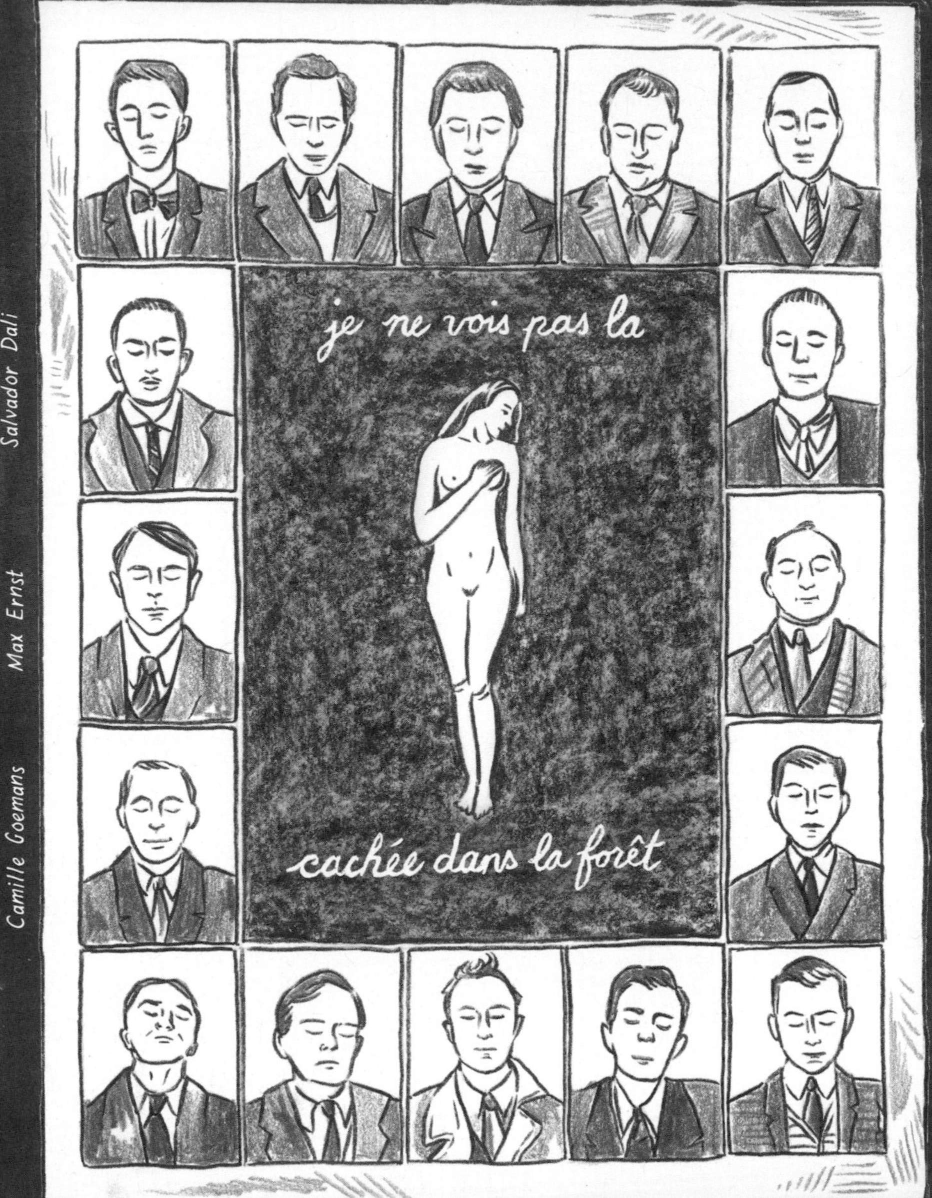

The European Surrealist movement did not officially allow women to join, but like most of art history, they used the female form liberally in their artworks.

There were actually many groups: artists, designers, collectors, that from the very start used the Photomaton in ways that Anatol hadn't envisioned.

Excerpt from December 15, 1928 issue of Variétés, a Belgian magazine.

"There are fanatics who collect hundreds of their 'expressions.' It is a system of psychoanalysis via image. The first strip surprises you as you struggle to find the individual you always believed yourself to be. After the second strip, and throughout all the many strips that follow, while you may do your best to play the superior individual, the original type, the dark fascinating one, or the monkey, none of the resulting visions will fully correspond to what you want to see in yourself."

Decades later, Andy Warhol's iconic use of photobooths associated the machines with the Pop Art movement.

Like others, Warhol saw photobooths as readymades. To him, they produced instant art and each photo was worthy of space on a gallery wall.

He used them obsessively from 1963-1966. In that time he took many portraits of himself and his celebrity friends.

Warhol's colourful screenprints of photostrips were featured on the cover of Time Magazine in 1965.

Anatol had conceived of the photobooth as a pleasant and simple way for people to photograph themselves. By the end of the 1920s, people had already found other uses for the machines for both practical and creative purposes.

By 1930, photobooths were used for official identity documents in many countries.

The new function of the machines bolstered the industry and transformed some photobooths from playful to serious spaces.

Many workplaces created I.D. badges by encasing photobooth pictures in pin back buttons.

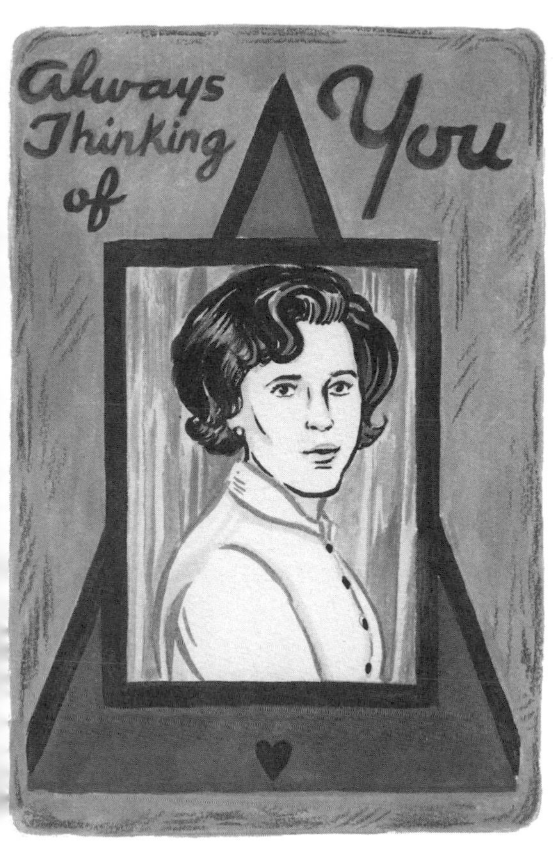

Photobooth related products and services flourished. Small frames were designed out of glass and metal or cardboard, to hold individual pictures.

Photobooth assistants would offer hand-tinting. When done expertly this made the photo appear to be in colour. Many people attemped to tint their photos themselves, often with sloppy results.

Cut-out forms to pose behind became popular for photobooths set up temporarily at carnivals and on boardwalks.

Photo-Weigh machines were found across Europe, particularly in Germany. There was a scale in the seat and a metre indicating your weight in front of the camera, as well as an automated calendar. Your image, weight and date were all captured.

John Slack, Photomaton employee, invented Movie Foto. It worked by taking three exposures on the same piece of paper, which you slid into an envelope that had a window made of lined acetate. When you shifted the image, you appeared to be animated.

Others tried optical tricks as well. There are records of at least two companies that made 3D photobooth pictures, visible when wearing the red and blue lensed glasses.

Not much is known about all the early, little companies that sprung up to get their own piece of the photobooth pie. Some of these short-lived business ventures had playful names to match their quirky gimmicks.

Some records of these companies exist, but the physical booths are long gone. They are remembered through the thousands of photos they produced.

Automatic Film Machine

AMERICAN PHOTOTURE

Tru-Photo Machine

PHOTOSNAP

PHOTOLA

QUARTERMATIC PHOTO MACHINE

NOW You Can Make Big Money on a small Investment!

PHOTA-STRIP JUNIOR

Greatest value ever offered in a direct positive photo machine! Strictly portable. Makes pictures 1½ x 2". Comes complete with precision-
built camera. F.3.5. Lens, automatic shutter,
all lighting arrangements and darkroom
facilities. Only.......................... **$140**

FREE CATALOG

MARKS & FULLER, INC.
Rochester NYC. USA

Patents are one of the ways we know about the range of businesses that were actually trying to advance the science of photobooths.

Patents weren't filed as "photobooths" however. Inventors came up with wordy, technical descriptions:

APPARATUS FOR DEVELOPING EXPOSED PHOTOGRAPHIC SURFACES

SENSITIZED PHOTOGRAPHIC CARD

Photographic machine for taking a negative and making a positive therefrom

MEANS FOR MAKING COMPOSITE PHOTOGRAPHS

Developing Appartus for Photographic Film Strip

The word "photobooth" was never coined by any particular company. It's so simple and straightforward, a sister-word to "phone booth," that it just somehow entered the lexicon and became widely accepted.

They studied the Photomatic's mechanics and business model and brainstormed a better photobooth. They returned to Anatol's strip format and conceived of simpler mechanisms, including a transmission and a cyclindrical interior, composed of fourteen baths, detailed at the start of this book.

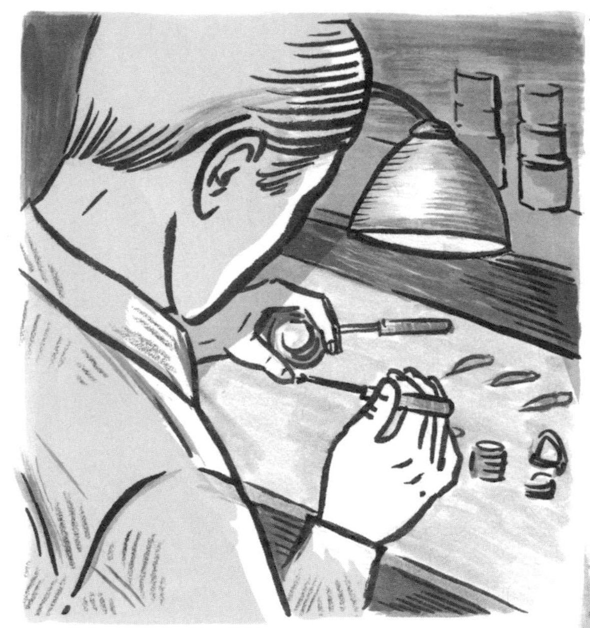

1946 Allen applied for a copyright and worked on a prototype, plainly named, the Model 7.

Baker found investors, started a mass-production plant in Los Angeles, and incorporated them as Auto-Photo.

Allen and Baker refined the Model 7 until they had something ready for the market. By 1950, they launched the Model 9, which was comparatively efficient and easy to service.

It was also a stunner, with art deco inspired details, curved sides, chrome trim and an interior enamel finish.

But the Model 9 had its faults. Salt from the chemicals rusted the mechanisms and a slow shutter speed often produced blurry photos. They hadn't developed the spider yet, with its seven arms, so it could only develop one strip every two and a half minutes.

A blurry photo of myself, taken in one of the last Model 9s.

The signage and the patterned curtain were not regular features, but extras for their debut.

Auto-Photo had a sharp vice-President, Van Nattan, who made a very clear business plan for the next few years.

In 1954, an English offshoot was formed and renamed Photo-Me Limited, bringing Auto-Photo's booths to the United Kingdom.

Improving the design further, in 1955, Auto-Photo launched the Model 11, adding a spider and switching flood lights for strobe lights, for crisper images.

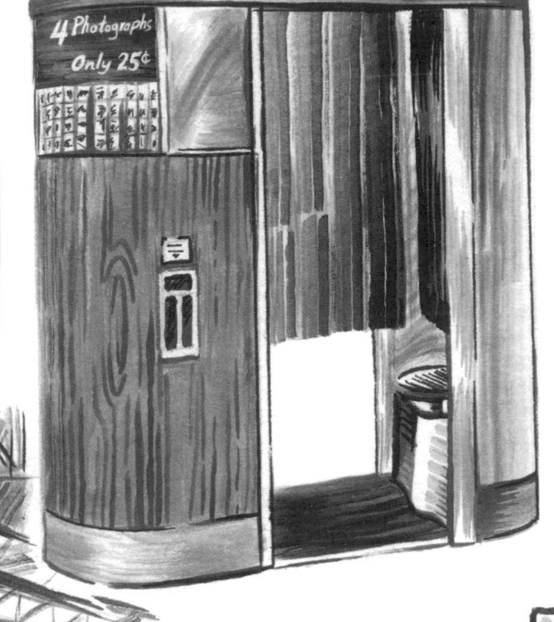

The Model 11 was a huge sensation and could be found just about anywhere. Photobooths were ideal for lovers, which facilitated complaints from other customers. Some owners put up preventative signs, while others just removed the exterior curtains.

The Model 11 became a fixture in pop culture.

In the opening sequence of the 1964 film *A Hard Day's Night*, three of the Beatles, John, Ringo and George hide inside a Model 11 in a train station to escape a crowd of adoring fans, while Paul hides behind a newspaper.

In the USA, Auto-Photo secured exclusive photobooth rights at cinemas, fairs and in train stations, as well as at Woolworths, the variety store chain. In 1962, in the UK, the company became Photo-Me International, establishing itself in other European countries. In 1963, a Japanese division, Nippon Auto-Photo Kabushiki Kaisha, formed to huge success.

In 1959 Auto-Photo launched the Model 12 and in 1964, the Model 14. These two models look identical. They were dependable, solid booths, with a boxy design that made them easier to ship and store than the curved designs of the former models. Aesthetically, they shifted from a feminine to a masculine feel.

Many of the B&W booths that are operational around the world today are Model 14s.

In 1966, several countries officially approved photobooth pictures for passport use, which sky-rocketed sales.

Model 12s produced a strip of only three photos. Model 14s produced four.

The Model 14 had a winged top, which unfortunately was often cut off for portability. A Model 14 today, without clipped wings, is a special find.

In 1974, Auto-Photo debuted the Model 17C, which was the first colour photobooth. Colour film for handheld cameras had technically been available since 1935 but was not affordable for the masses until nearly 1970.
In the mid-80s, Photo-Me International bought the original American Auto-Photo Company, which became Photo-Me USA.
Photographies en
COLOR PHOTOGRAPHS COULEUR
PHOTOGRAPHIES EN COULEUR
COLOR PHOTOGRAPHS
75¢
2 PHOTOS 4 MINUTES
This French Canadian booth produced two photos for $0.75.
By 1989, Photo-Me International and its subsidiaries operated more than 15,000 photobooths in more than 100 countries.
COLOR
COLOR
3
$1.50
4½ MINUTES

4 Different Poses
IN COMPLETE PRIVACY
Only 25¢
PHOTOS DELIVERED HERE
IN 2½ MINUTES
PLATFORM
11
auto-PHOTO
MODEL 11
RARE

14

By 2008, I had a couple thousand pictures.
I divided my collection into three parts:

1. Self-Portraits
2. Donated
3. Found.

While most of the pictures were of myself, I was more interested in pictures of other people. I asked friends to send me photobooth pictures of themselves and I received many heartwarming and hysterical photos.

I could begin to see relationships between the photos. Through the patterns that emerged, I began to see universal types of photobooth behaviour...

in my own family...

My dad in 1972.

My younger brother, Kieran, in 2007.

My youngest brother, Tiegh, in 2005.

...and in strangers.

The treasures of my collection were my found photos, they were rare and precious.

I often made up elaborate back stories to explain why they looked the way they did and how the photos ended up getting lost or left behind.

Narratives naturally emerge from four sequential images. I found it easy to get lost in other people's lives.

← *Photos from four different strips that I found in a six month period, in and around photobooths. Coincidentally, all of the girls appear to be First Nations.*

I acquired my favourite found photograph in 2005.

Emily and I were standing near a booth, waiting for the couple inside to finish. When their pictures were ready, the man rushed to grab them. He shielded them from his girlfriend and tore the third picture out of the strip, then ripped it into pieces and threw into in the garbage bin. He told his girlfriend it was because his eyes were closed.

Emily and I knew we'd be recovering the pieces once they left. She let me keep it.

In those early years, the quantity of photos mattered to me almost as much as the quality. I felt so much pleasure logging new photos and tallying up my total.

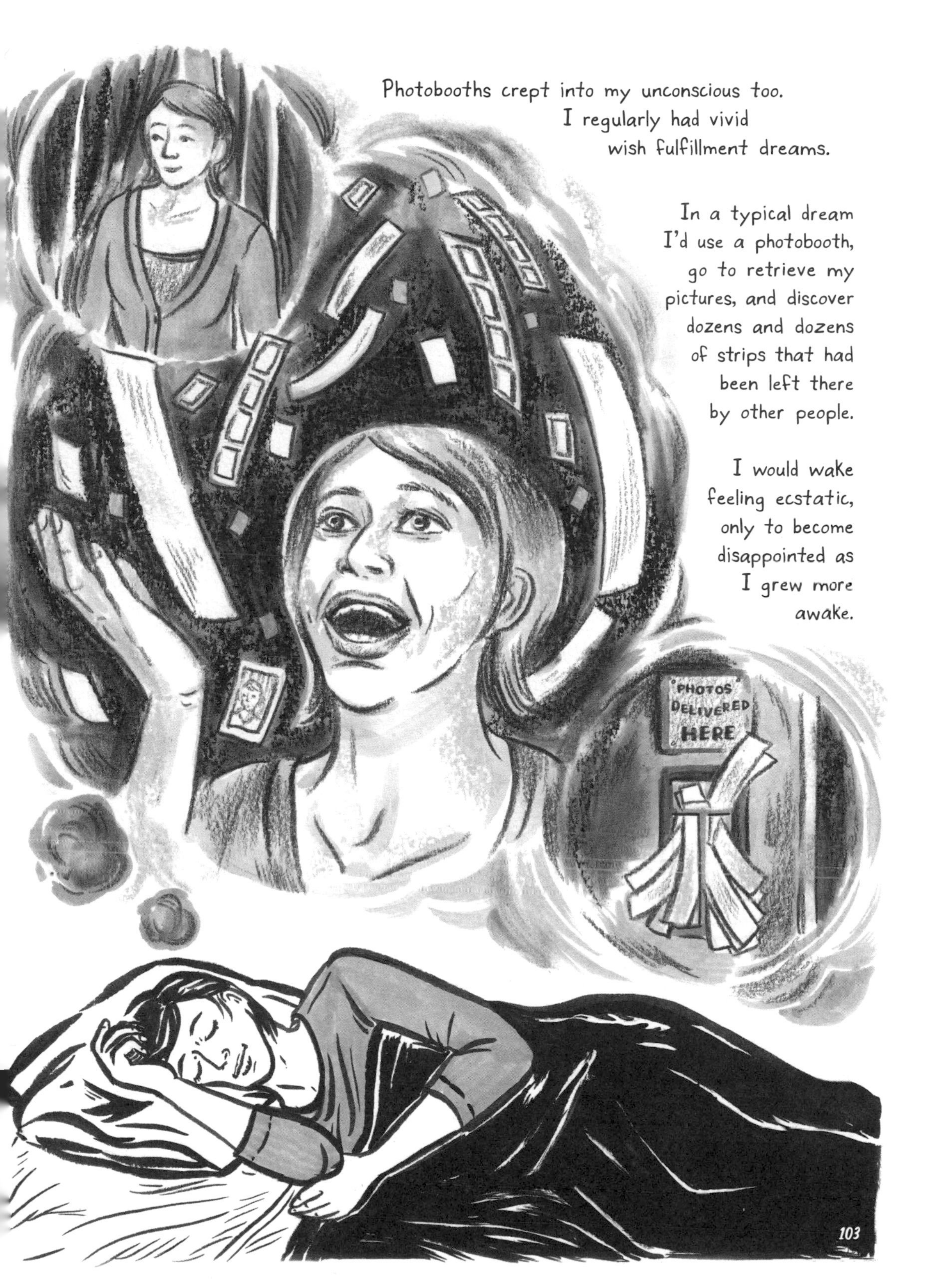
Photobooths crept into my unconscious too. I regularly had vivid wish fulfillment dreams.
In a typical dream I'd use a photobooth, go to retrieve my pictures, and discover dozens and dozens of strips that had been left there by other people.
I would wake feeling ecstatic, only to become disappointed as I grew more awake.
PHOTOS DELIVERED HERE

15
1923
GRAFLEX SERIES B
The photobooth industry's history is simple when compared to the vast hand-held camera industry from the same period.
The Photomaton, the Photomatic and Auto-Photo were leaders, but were generally exceptions in the industry. Like the major camera companies, they were legitimate and law abiding.
SPARTUS PRESS FLASH
1939
SPARTUS PRESS FLASH
TIME
INST.
CHICAGO ILLINOIS USA
Smaller photobooth owners didn't make all of their decisions in a board room. If it was a slow day for business, maybe a booth owner would pay a kid to visit the other photobooths in the area and jam their coin slots with washers. The vending world played by its own rules.
1947
ANSCO PLENAX PB 20
PLENAX
20 PLENAX
History has favoured big business. But there are likely hundreds of stories of short term, one or two booth operations that will never be told.
BROWNIE BULLS EYE
1954
Brownie
BULL'S-EYE
Camera
KODAK TWINDAR
POLAROID SWINGER
1965
POLAROID
LAND CAMERA
SWINGER
MODEL 20

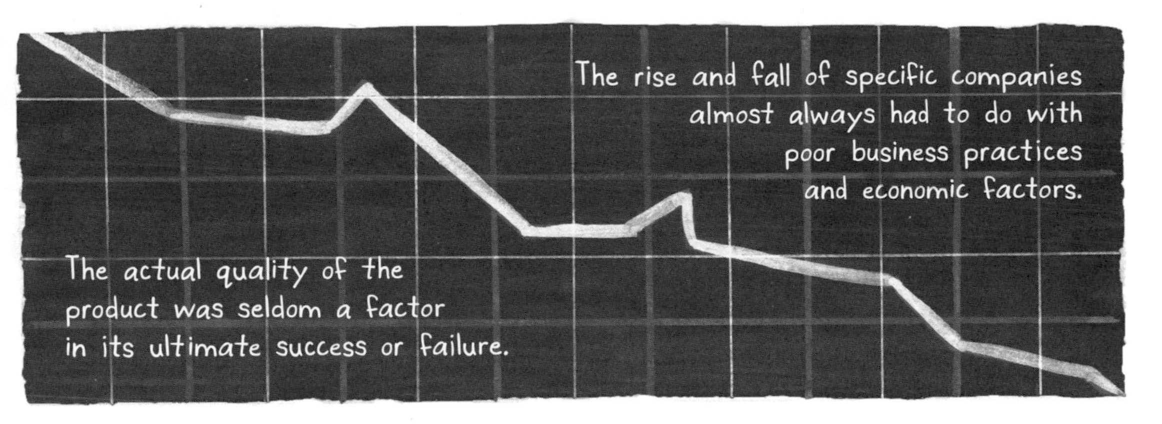

The Photomatic went under when the President of the Mutoscope Reel Company died in an accident, followed by the deaths of two other executives, which left the company in the hands of Marty Rabkin, the President's young and inexperienced son.

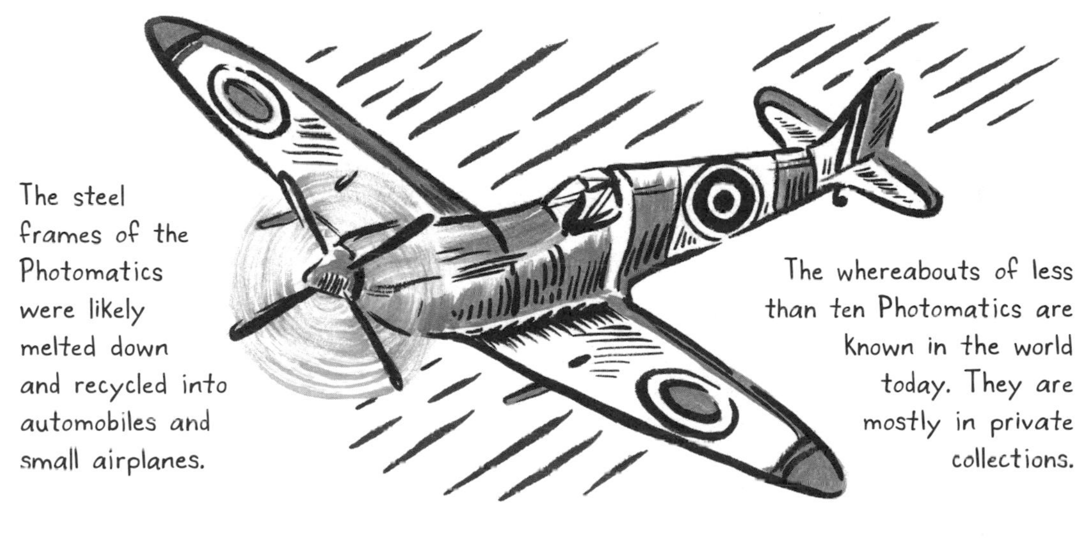

The steel frames of the Photomatics were likely melted down and recycled into automobiles and small airplanes.

The whereabouts of less than ten Photomatics are known in the world today. They are mostly in private collections.

The smaller companies couldn't compete with Auto-Photo's and Photo-Me's superior business models.

Nearly all the photobooths from these failed businesses went to landfills and scrap metal yards. Almost none of these thousands exist today.

The industry in Canada was jolted in 1968, when the purported assassin of Martin Luther King Jr., James Earl Ray, fled to Toronto and nearly escaped to England with a false Canadian passport. In response, Canada tightened its passport regulations to exclude photobooth pictures, despite the fact that his photo was taken at a studio.

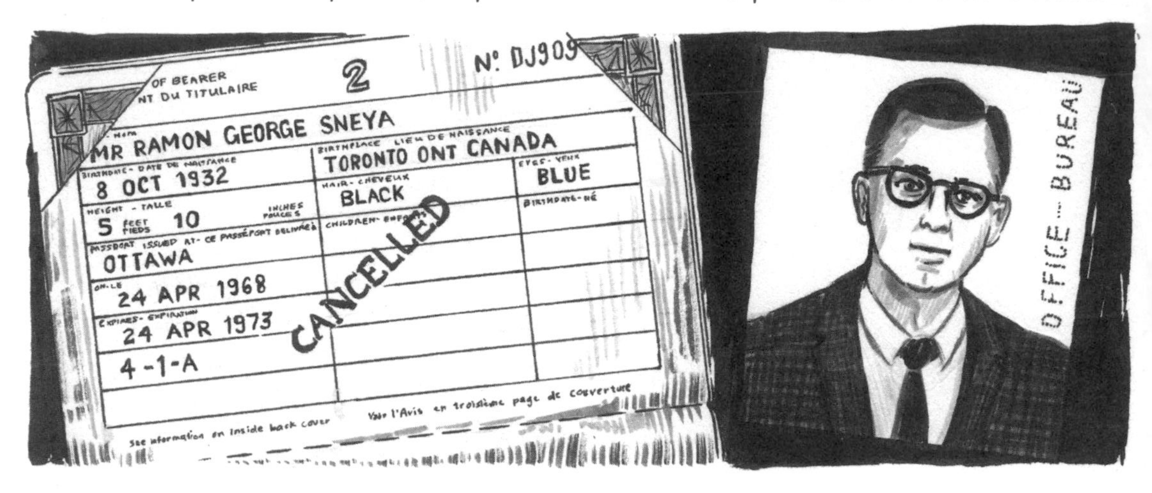

Other criminals did take advantage of the private nature of photobooths.

Throughout his "career," French criminal, Jacques Mesrine, guilty of bank robberies, burglaries, kidnapping and murder in multiple countries, used photobooth pictures in his falsified documents from 1966 to 1979. He was coined *The Man of a Thousand Faces* for his disguises and many successful attempts at escaping prison.

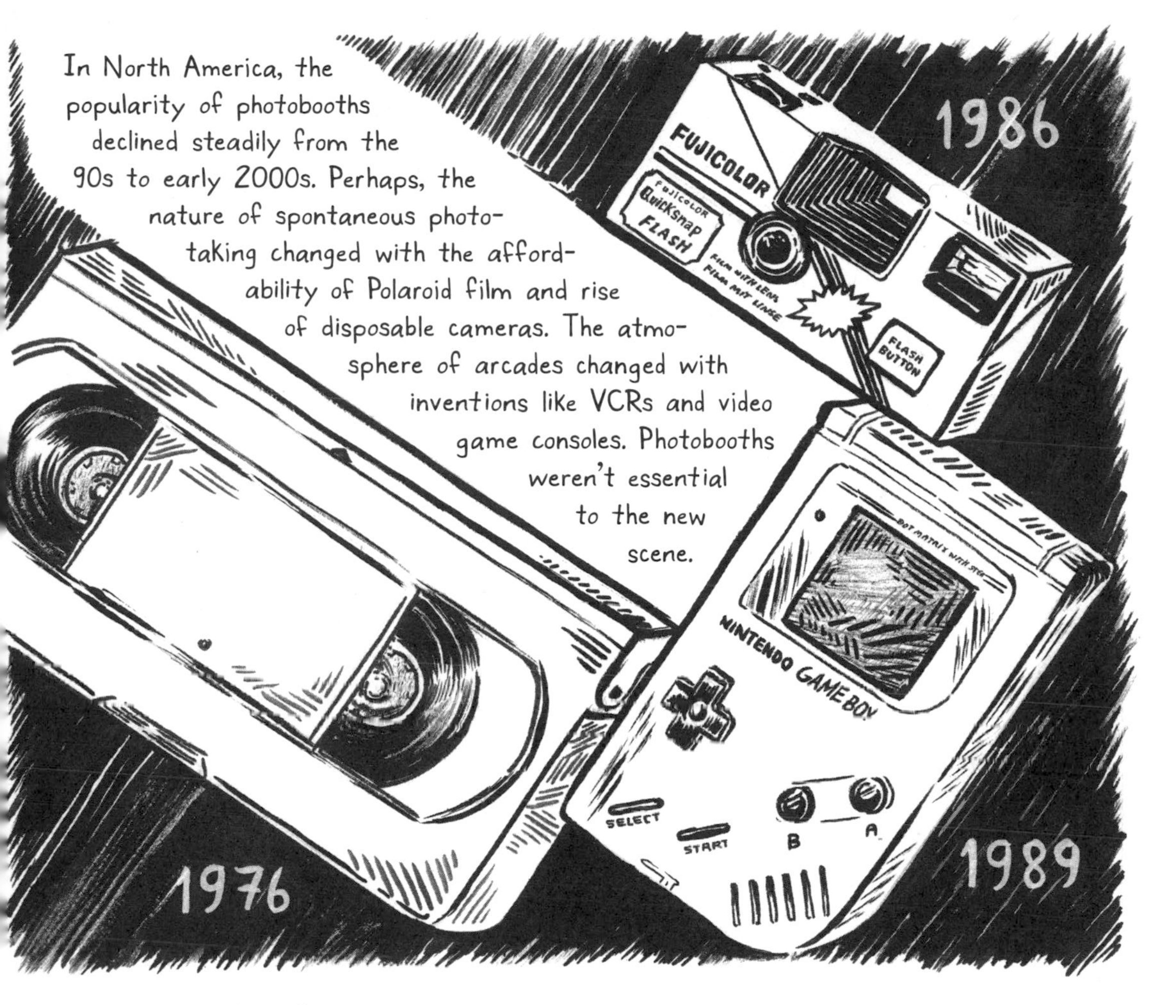

But the largest factor was the digital era.

Photo-Me International was an early adoptor of the new technology, despite the inferior quality of the early digital photobooths. Their first digital booth was unveiled in 1994.

The transition years were awkward, pitting the old, reliable booths against the new, glitchy ones.

Lots of innovation and hard work paid off for a few deserving individuals in the industry.
The fruits of their labours were obvious.
Today, those who are committed to the mechanics and chemistry face many challenges.
Sadly, in recent years several key figures in the old industry have passed away...
and with them, irrecoverable history and knowledge as well.
Time, not competition, is now the largest contributing factor against the continued existence of these analog machines.
FIFTY PENCE
50
25 cents

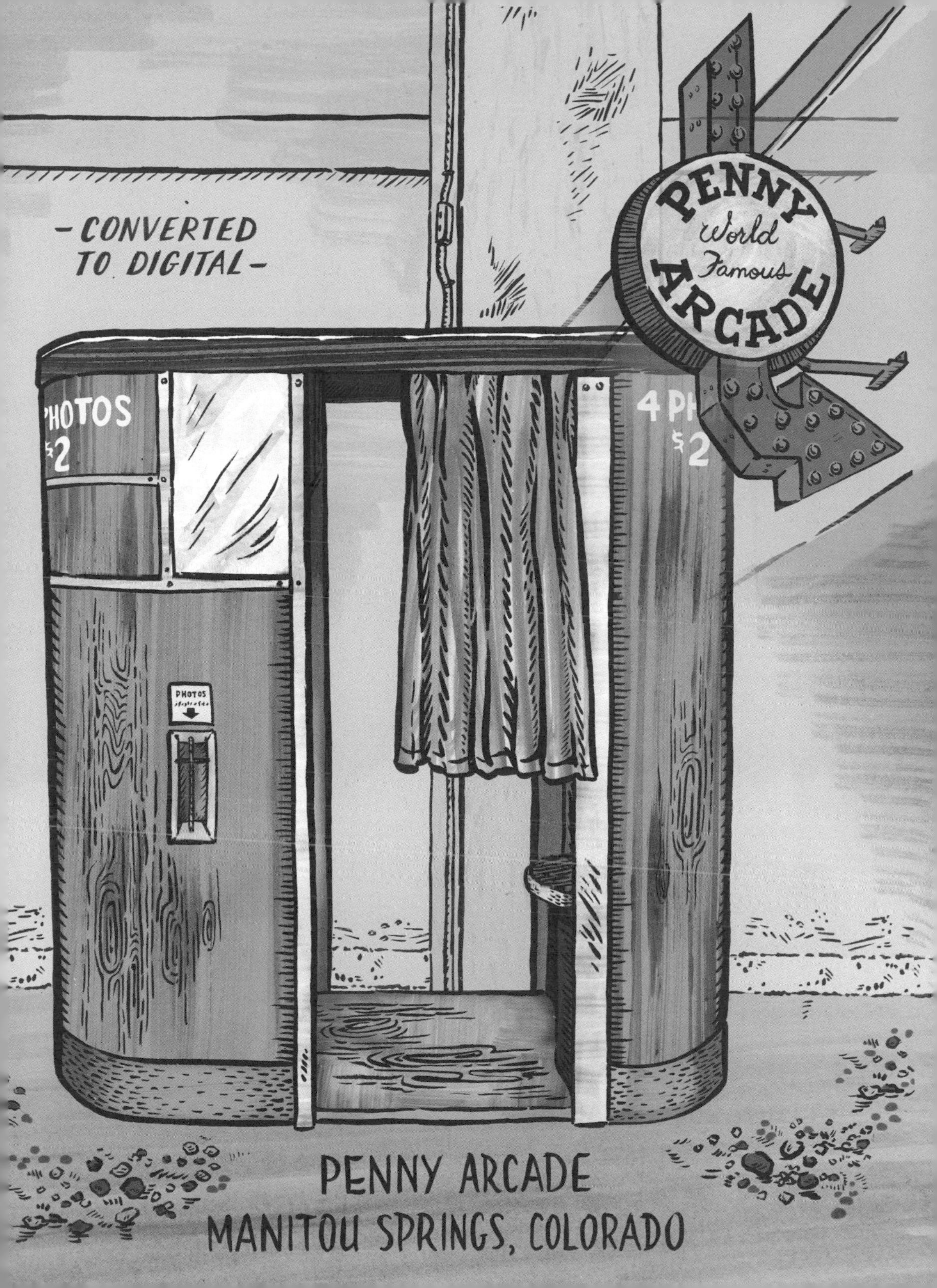
-CONVERTED TO DIGITAL-
PENNY
World Famous
ARCADE
PHOTOS
$2
4 PH
$2
PHOTOS
PENNY ARCADE
MANITOU SPRINGS, COLORADO

PART II

Photobooths didn't die, they evolved, and not just into digital photobooths.

Their spirit lives on in photo editing software and in apps.

The term photobooth has come to mean new things. It's been broadened to refer to an area of a party where a digital camera on a tripod is set up to take photos of people wearing costumes and holding props. I think that is better described as a "photo station."

The word "photobooth" is thrown around very casually now.

If you type in "photobooth props" into a search engine, you'll see that a new market has emerged to provide people with paper mustaches, goofy glasses and oversized lips.

The evolution of technology is to be expected, but some of us just can't let go of the old stuff.

Before 2005, a few people had attempted to make lists of the remaining chemical photobooths and some forums formed so photobooth fans could find one another. These early websites were crudely designed and not reliably updated.

But obviously there was a need for such a database and the companies owning the chemical booths were too busy getting rid of them to create or contribute to a master list.

TIM GARRETT

- computer scientist
- photobooth artist
- has the same birthday as me

BRIAN MEACHAM

- film preservationist
- a 2011, four-time Jeopardy champion. He bought a photobooth with winnings

In January 2005, Tim sent Brian an email proposing that they combine their efforts. They laid out a vision for a website that tracked all chemical photobooth sightings in all media and would have a worldwide locator feature. The next day Brian responded enthusiastically and contributed the idea of a multi-authored blog to the mix.

The whole concept of Photobooth.net was encompassed in those first two emails. Tim wrote the custom code for the technical workings of the website while Brian compiled the content. Less than five months later, the website was up!

With some momentum behind them, in May 2005, Brian and Tim hosted an International Photobooth Convention at the Mad Art Gallery in St. Louis.

There had been a convention in 2004 in Belgrade and in 2003 in New York City. The ones before those had all been in the United Kingdom.

Brian described the site to me as a very broad look at a very narrow subject. Its archives keep track of photobooth sightings across all forms of media.

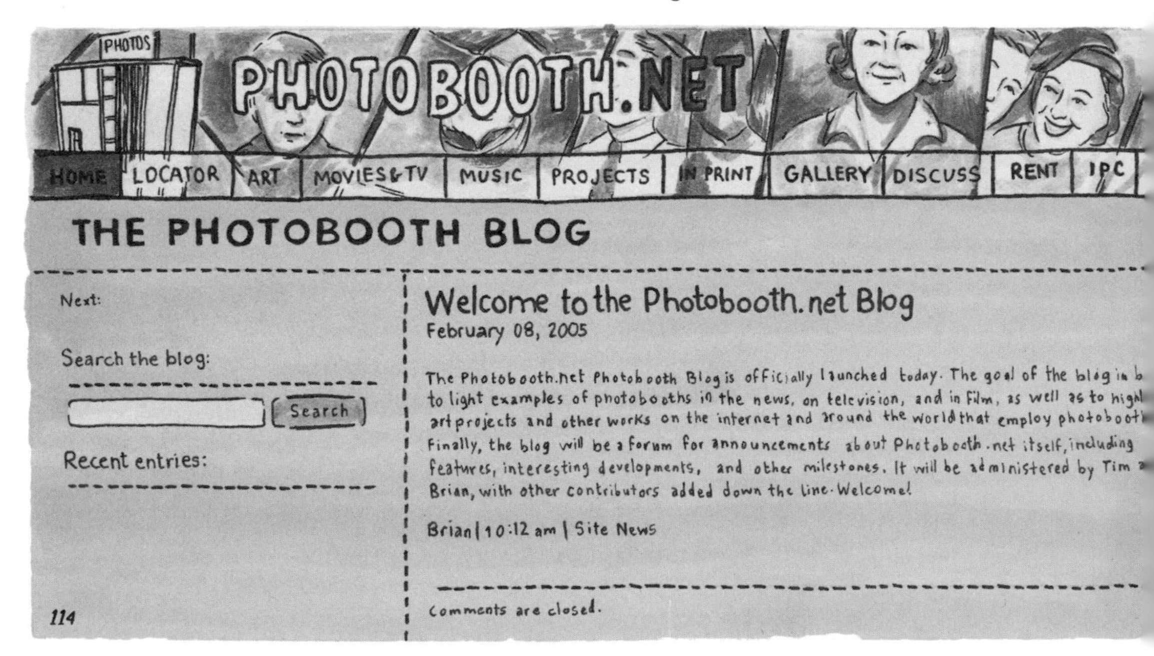

Photobooth enthusiasts from around the world were looking for each other and Photobooth.net became the perfect hub. International connections and friendships formed and contributions to the various databases started to come in.
And their timing in 2005 was pretty perfect. Auto-Photo Canada, Photo-Me USA, and other companies started to rid their warehouses of their old chemical photobooths. A grassroots movement formed as people from all backgrounds—artists, mechanics, entrepreneurs—bought these old machines and planned to operate them themselves.
Now, almost all the chemical photobooths in the world are operated by these small businesses, run by people who had no previous experience in the photobooth industry.
Photobooth.net is still at the core of this community today.

It's been almost a decade since Tim and Brian started the site and they've observed how the photobooth scene has changed for better and for worse.

PHOTOBOOTH FANS CREATING DEMAND

COMPANIES DIVESTING

"There's an amazing disconnect between the businesses who have supplied these machines and the people who love them. The businesses can't wait to get rid of them, with their constant breakdowns and nasty chemicals, and the photobooth devotees will do anything they can to hold on to them. Just as businesses divest themselves of these machines, people are realizing they could go away, and they need to hold on to these booths as tightly as they can."

— Brian

In the summer of 2012, Tim described this graph to me.

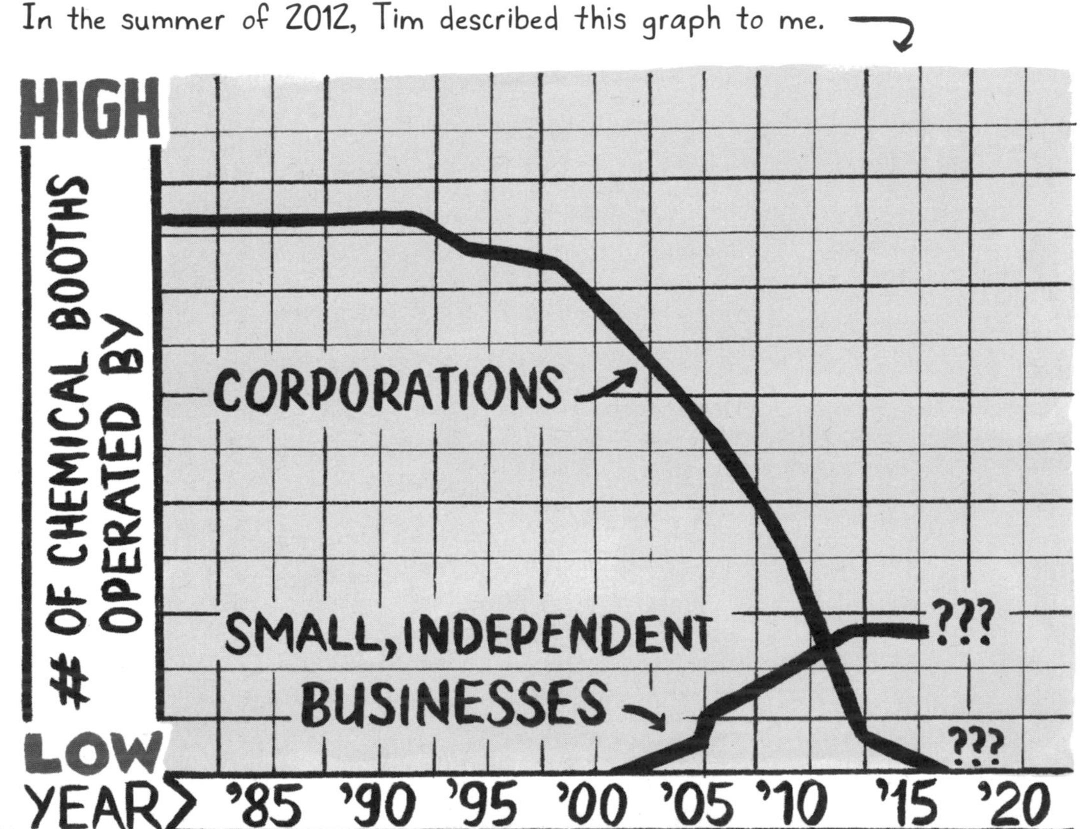

Photobooth.net has been an essential source for these new photobooth owners who need to figure out how to operate a machine without formal training. Owners from across the world can share resources and tips.

At one time the website mainly chronicled media, writings and past events. The website now shares upcoming events, somewhat changing the purpose and feel of it.

The community continues to expand.

The locator feature is a huge database of information about booths from around the world. This database is great for both the traveling photobooth fan who wants to find locations for the city they're visiting, and also for the booth owners who can increase their visibility by being listed.

2006 I found Photobooth.net and was surprised to see that so few Canadian booths had been listed on the Locator. A few booths in Toronto and Montreal were listed, but the rest of the country was unrepresented.

I thought this was odd, considering that Canada had so many booths, because Auto-Photo Canada, unlike their American equivalents hadn't yet made the massive switch to digital.

Later I realized that it's because Canada had so many photobooths that no one was sending in locations.

Generally, Canadians are not nostalgic for photobooths because they can still occasionally be found in public places. There hasn't been a chance to get heart-sick for them, so nothing has spurred on an indie business movement.

I started to keep lists of the booths I was using. I photographed them and noted their serial and model numbers, as well as any unique traits.

2009 Finally, after years of diligently tracking every photobooth I visited, often going out of my way to find new ones, in August I made my first direct contact with Photobooth.net. I sent a list of 25 or so locations. For some reason, I was very shy and nervous about it.

Hi Brian,
Here are some locations that hopefully you can use for the website.
cheers,
Meags Fitzgerald

I realized later that it was probably very strange for him to receive a clump of listings like that. When I became less shy, I sent them in one or two at a time.

It was on Photobooth.net that I first saw very good photobooth art made by professional artists.

Four of the five artists presented in Concerning the Photobooth at Museet for Fotokunst, Odense, Denmark in 2001.

LEFT TO RIGHT:
Liz Rideal (UK)
Herman Costa (USA)
Jan Wenzel (GER)
Cendrillon Bélanger (FR)

I realized that it was possible to take photobooths out of their "everydayness" and use them to make beautiful and clever artwork.

I hadn't been thinking far enough outside of the box with my own work and hadn't shown my professors or peers what was so special about the format.

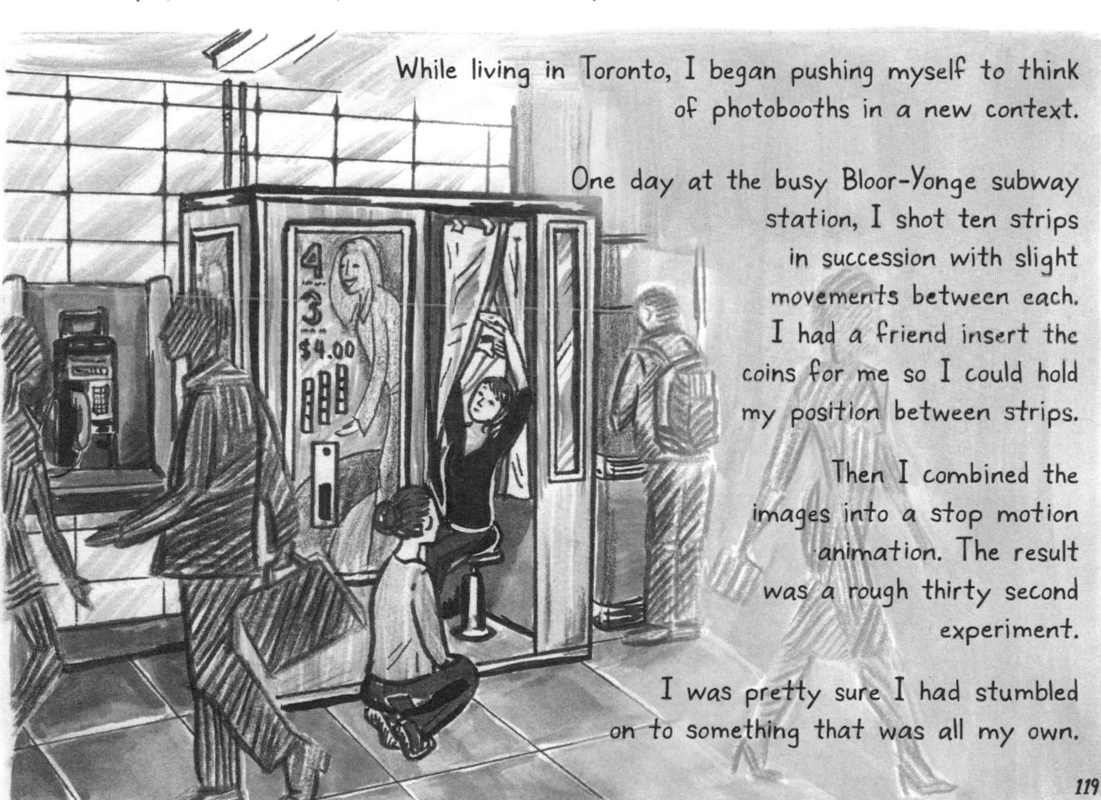

DRAKE HOTEL
TORONTO

--EXTINCT-- *replaced by digital*

17 Back in Calgary for the last year of my degree, I took a class in curatorial studies and cultures of display. We studied practices and theories behind collecting.

I've been a collector of things my whole life.

At nine years old I was determined not to share a room with my sister any longer. Without consulting my parents, I moved my bedroom into our unfinished basement. I became obsessed with making my dungeon-like bedroom more hospitable, in part by putting up posters of cats, and only of cats. I aspired to be surrounded *floor to ceiling* by cats.

Today I collect unused vintage air mail envelopes from all over the world in a range of languages, colours and patterns.

And picture frames, specifically cast iron oval frames with beveled glass made in Italy between 1930-50.

In the class we talked about the ways of displaying collections and how the display method and subject equally convey the collection's significance.

Unlike my other collections on display, my photobooth pictures were private, stored in archival plastic and zipped up in leather binders.

I wondered why collectors like myself take pleasure in acquiring multiples of one type of thing? Was it the product or the process I was obsessed with?

I've never gambled, but I can see the similarities between

A PHOTOBOOTH & A SLOT MACHINE.

Each of the steps—inserting money, striking poses/pulling down a lever, waiting for the outcome and getting good or bad photos/winning or losing money—produce similar habit-forming adrenaline rushes.

If two out of four photos in a strip are great, I consider the strip a success. If all four photos turn out very well it's like hitting the jackpot.

The best known photobooth collection belongs to the French writer, Michel Folco. His albums of found photobooth pictures served as inspiration for Jean-Pierre Jeunet, director of the film *Amélie* for the character Nino Quincampoix.

"The potential inwardness of objects is one of their most powerful characteristics, ambiguous and elusive though it may be. Objects hang before the eyes of the imagination, continuously re-presenting ourselves to ourselves, and telling the stories of our lives in ways which would be impossible otherwise."

– SUSAN M. PEARCE
Museums, Objects And Collections

Collecting is about telling a story. It's told through what we choose to collect, by the objects we select and don't select for our collections, and by how we share or don't share them with the world.

Personally, I feel like collecting is about making a commitment to the material world. My collections are mostly of antiques and vintage items. For me collecting them is a way of preserving them. Photobooth pictures are an exception to this, the photos are new of course, but the format makes them instantly feel genuinely old. By taking the pictures, I preserve myself.

A collector is motivated by an instinct initially unrelated to objects. I could see this in myself when I realized that I was also collecting experiences.
June 2005
June 2004
July 2007
June 2006
By 2004, my friend Emily and I recognized how important those silly pictures we took on June 23, 2003 were to kicking off my collection, so we decided to re-enact them on the same day, in the same photobooth, in the same clothes. It became a tradition and we found a way, despite the physical distance between us, to re-enact the originals once or twice a year ever since.
June 2008
December 2009
December 2010
May 2013

18

2009

In the spring, I finished my degree, a Bachelor's of Fine Arts. My exams and final evaluations wrapped up right around my birthday, April 26th.

The next day I got an unexpected phone call, offering me an improv teaching opportunity in Sydney, Australia. It was technically volunteer work but all my expenses were paid and there was an honorarium.

I said "Yes!" of course, and all of a sudden my life was on a whole other trajectory, from academia to airports. I didn't know it then but the trip to Australia kicked off eighteen months of international travel, mostly with teaching and performing improv.

MODERN ART HISTORY 1920-1965

Glasses I bought with the money I saved up for a tattoo.

UNITED AIRLINES

A $15 sandwich, bought on an airplane.

Noise cancelling head-phones.

TRUTH IN COMEDY

Life was a whirlwind.
My evenings were spent in comedy clubs and in make-shift theatres...
...or driving between cities in a tour van or on Greyhound buses, or in airports, waiting for connecting flights.
While on the road, I forfeited my studio and was drifting away from my fine arts practice. Perhaps naturally, photobooths took the spotlight again.
In every city I visited I tried to find all the photobooths I could and document them for Photobooth.net's locator.

TAKE YOUR OWN PHOTO
TRAVEL PASS
FUN PHOTOS
LOVED ONES
$8
$1 OR $2
COINS
ONLY
I.D.
SCHOOL
SPORT
4 Black and White Photos in 3 Minutes
ACCEPTS 1 & 2 COINS
PHOTOS
Q BAR
SYDNEY
-ACTIVE-

Sometimes, I told Brian which cities I'd be visiting and he would send me any tips he had received for booths in those areas. I always tried to find time amidst my work schedule to visit them.
-ATIONS:
-G MALLS:
COLOUR -EAST GARDEN
-PARRAMATTA
B&W -MIRANDA
-LIVERPOOL
-HURSTVILLE
Other times, I would arrive in a new city and just ask locals, sometimes strangers on the street, if they knew where any photobooths were. With this strategy, I was often directed to digital booths. I realized that most people had never considered the difference.
While visiting my friend Cari in Ottawa, we called the phone number we found in a local photobooth and just asked the technician for the list of booths he serviced.
This diminished some of the thrill of the treasure hunt, but it was very efficient since I was constantly changing cities.
BOOTHS
-St. Laurent Shopping Cent.
-llings Bridge Centre
-Central bus station

4 POSES
FINISH
2 MIN
PHOTO
HOLD STILL
RAYKO PHOTO CENTER
SAN FRANCISCO
AUTO-PHOTO MODEL 9
-active-

I returned to Sydney in the summer of 2010 and by then I had developed some better booth hunting strategies.

The booths were mostly in bars and were very pricey, and when I visited at night, I had to pay a cover charge just to get in. So, I called the bars ahead of time, telling them I *worked* for Photobooth.net. They usually let me visit during the daytime and sometimes let me take free photos too!

In 2010, Photo-Me International was still running the last of their chemical booths in shopping malls. Other small companies were operating chemical booths in nightclubs and bars.

Many B&W Australian booths produce sepia toned photos and have a long six seconds between taking the photos.

A model that is completely foreign to me in a shopping mall in Glebe, Sydney.

← Photostrip from the Cargo bar. The booth overlapped the images where the border was meant to be.
While in Australia, I didn't get a chance to visit Melbourne but some friends told me about a few Model 18s that were still operational there. These Model 18s took a strip of three long photos.
My friend Victoria in a Model 18.
BLACK and WHITE PHOTOS $4 POSES
PHOTOS
Take your own photo
3 poses
$4
They were owned and serviced by an industry veteran, Alan Adler who bought his first booths in the early 1970s. At one time Alan operated sixteen booths in the area but his business has dwindled over the years.
A well-loved, outdoor booth on Chapel Street in Prahran, Melbourne.

I learned that shyness didn't serve me. I could accomplish a lot by just asking.

Otto's SHRUNKEN HEAD

NEW YORK CITY

-INACTIVE-

In Berlin, I found photobooths outside, despite it being winter. The booths, which are owned and serviced by an indie company, Photoautomat, use their own secret chemical formula, resulting in crisp, high contrast photos.

In recent years, Berlin has become a photobooth mecca. Photoautomat is making a strong and successful effort to revive chemical photobooths. The booths are outside and all over the city, the whole thing feels Kinda badass.

Square photos from Marienberg, Berlin

Berlin was the first place, but not the last, that I found booths that smelt like urinals and had collected the detritus of sex and drug use.

In Paris, I found booths by another indie company, Fotoautomat France, that were expertly refurbished and placed in art galleries and in cultural spaces.

REMEMBER NOT TO SPEND ANY CHANGE. SAVE IT FOR THE BOOTHS.

I WONDER IF EVERYONE IN THE TOUR VAN WOULD BE WILLING TO STOP TO CHECK OUT THAT ARCADE.

My focus shifted from collecting photobooth pictures to collecting photobooths.

Similarly to how I wanted floor to ceiling cat posters as a child, I now wanted to use every photobooth.

I'M HAVING A TERRIBLE HAIR DAY. I DON'T WANT TO HAVE MY PICTURE TAKEN BUT I HAVE THREE BOOTHS TO VISIT TODAY.

THAT BOOTH IS ONLY A COUPLE HOURS AWAY. I SHOULD TRY TO VISIT.

KOTTBUSSER TOR
KREUZBERG BERLIN active

PARIS
PALAIS DE TOKYO
ACTIVE

Digital identity photos I took in a train station in a Photo-Me International booth.

In 2010, I went to Tokyo, where chemical photobooths are long extinct. It was Japanese companies after all, that developed the first software for digital booths. The culture surrounding these, now very advanced digital photobooths, is like nowhere else in the world.

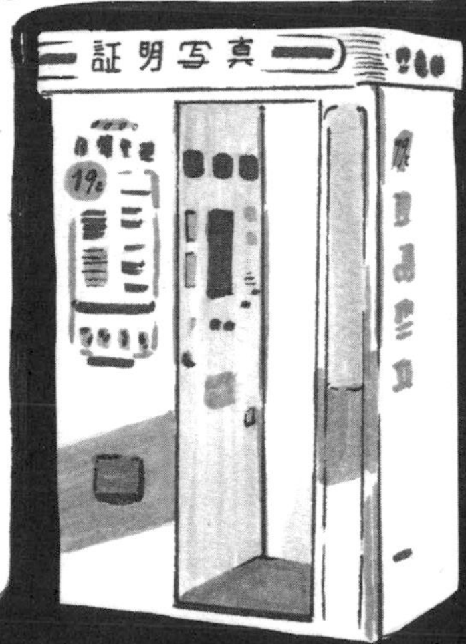

The sensation is called "puriKura" and every teenage girl in Japan has participated in it.

The photobooths produce images in a variety of sized images, including sheets of miniature stickers, which are collected and traded. The software allows you to make enhancements, like enlarging your eyes and decorating your scene.

↑ *Purikura photos my brother took with a friend in Japan in 2013, despite that this booth was "for girls only." His eyes are extra pretty.*

The international travel made me feel a bit like Anatol as he searched for the right resources, place and time to launch his invention. Decades later, I was visiting faraway places in search of descendants of his invention.

Based in my hometown of Edmonton, Jeff and I were able to meet up in person to discuss a photobooth art contest he wanted to host on his website. He asked if I would be one of the judges. I said yes and a whole little world opened up.

2011
I loved improv but the traveling was taking its toll. Increasingly, I began to see myself as an introvert in groups of extroverts. Performing on demand became more and more difficult.
So, in January, wanting a clean slate, I moved to Halifax, never having visited the Maritimes before.

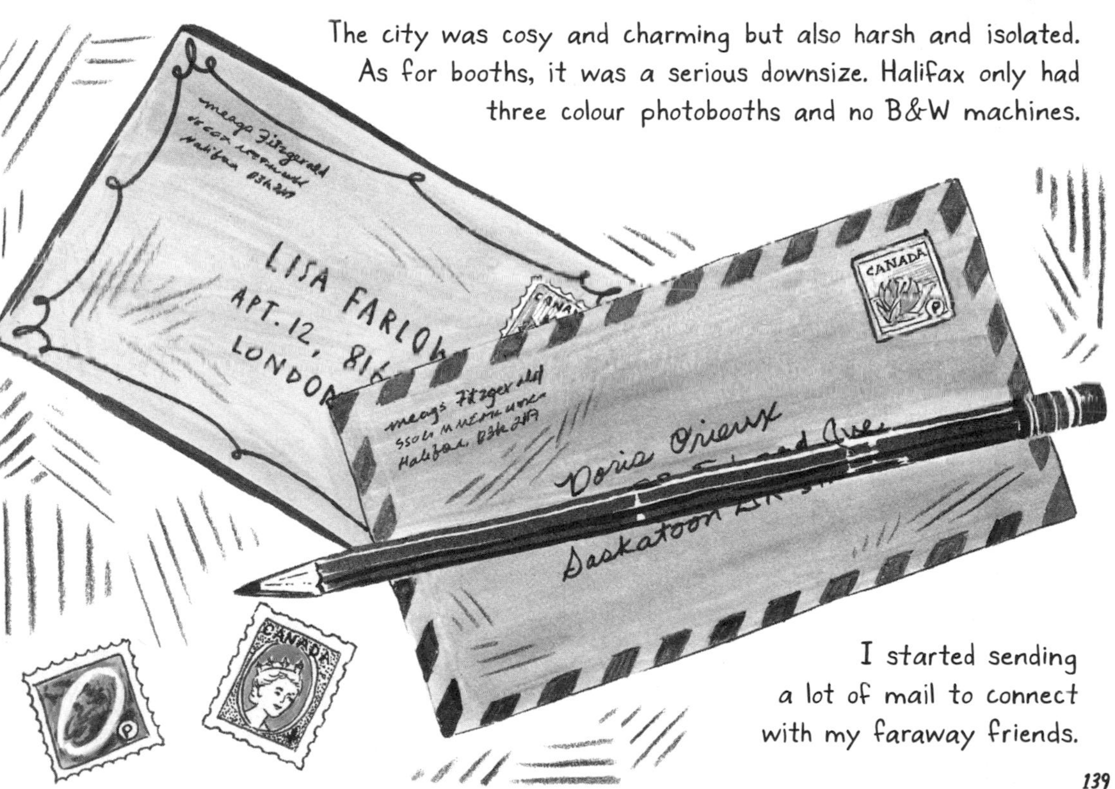
The city was cosy and charming but also harsh and isolated. As for booths, it was a serious downsize. Halifax only had three colour photobooths and no B&W machines.
LISA FARLO
APT. 12,
LONDO
CANADA
Doris Orieux
Saskatoon
CANADA
I started sending a lot of mail to connect with my faraway friends.

As a side project, I came up with the Photobooth Drawing Swap, as a way for my collection to continue to grow.
MEAGS
MEAGS
It was simple. People, mostly strangers, would send me photobooth pictures of themselves in the mail
FITZGERALD
NICOLE
JOEL
NORAH
and in exchange I would send them a couple of drawings.
MAIL
There was a five month period that I received a hand-addressed envelope in the mail every day of the week. It felt like Christmas everytime I opened my mail box!
People seemed to like the drawings, so I decided to take a stab at freelance illustration.

ACTIVE

Scotia Square HALIFAX

20 **2012**

I was back at University, this time to do a one year certificate in design. In February, while working in the computer lab, I saw that Photobooth.net had announced the next International Photobooth Convention. It was only three months away in Venice, California!

I stopped myself from jumping up and down in the computer lab. I was thrilled but immediately perplexed at how I would get there. I was a totally broke student.

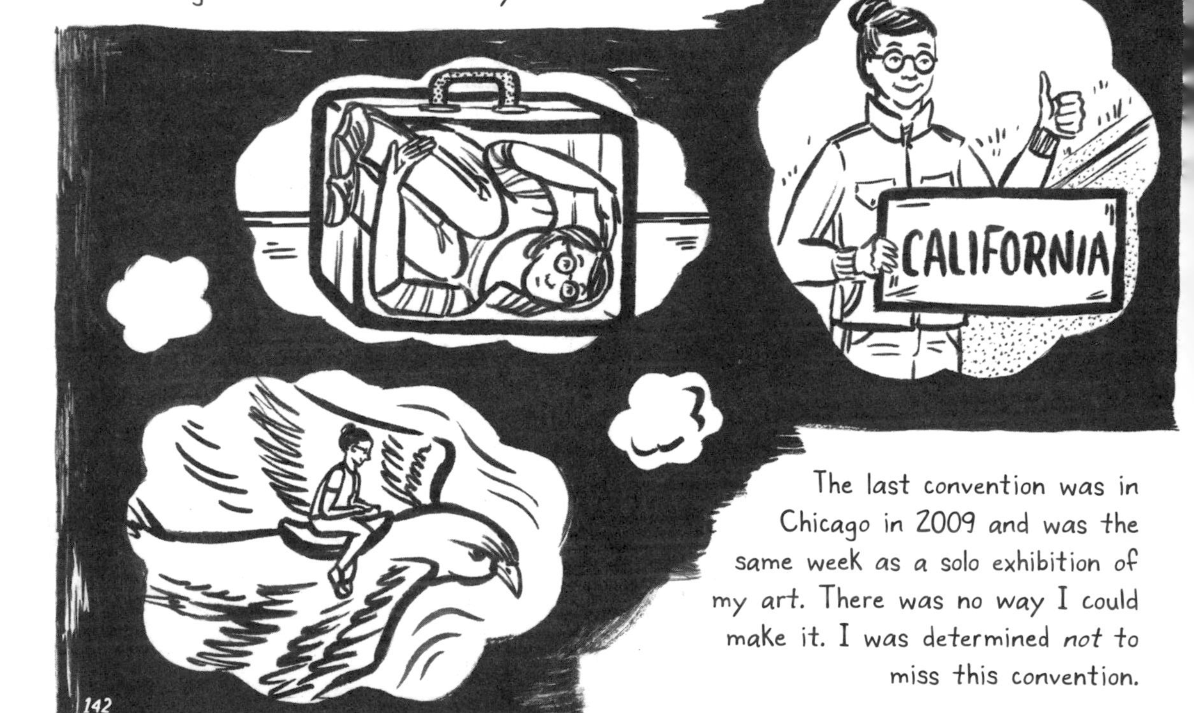

The last convention was in Chicago in 2009 and was the same week as a solo exhibition of my art. There was no way I could make it. I was determined *not* to miss this convention.

I came up with an idea to raise the money and put a plan into action.

In the daytime I did my school work and the occasional illustration job, and at night I used the school's facilities to design, print, silkscreen, and sew various items that I would offer as rewards to people who donated to my cause.

I fell silly about asking for the money just so I could go on vacation. So I decided that I would make a 32 page comic* with what I learned at the convention and later, at a visit to Auto-Photo Canada's warehouse in Montreal.

In April I was finally ready to launch a crowd source fundraiser. I called it the Photobooth Expedition. My goal was to raise $2,500 in three weeks.

So, I was delighted when I received $3,737 and lots of encouragement!

Silkscreening with my super friend Krista at 4 AM so we could have the facilties to ourselves.

* That little comic turned into this book. I had no idea what I was getting into.

Everything clicked into place and serendipity took care of my trip plans.

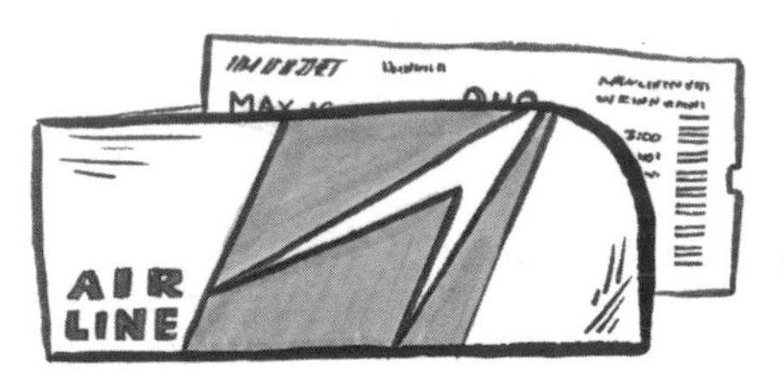

Silkscreened tote bags were one of the donor rewards.

▶ A friend who was working for an airline and gave me buddy passes to cover part of my airfare.

▶ A worldly photographer, Corbin and his partner, Paul heard about my campaign and offered to host me in their gorgeous house in Venice. They lived only a five minute walk from the beach and a ten minute walk from the convention venue!

▶ Tyler and John, friends from a high school improv competition, now filmmakers in Los Angeles, also offered me their apartment for my stay after the convention. They were able to give me their house keys in person because by crazy coincidence they arrived in Halifax on business the day before I left for California. We hadn't seen each other in years and we caught up in their hotel lobby.

▶ To top it off, my old friend, Kory agreed to fly to L.A. and accompany me for the convention.

>>>>>>> I graduated from my program and boarded an airplane for Los Angeles.

The concept of a photobooth convention evolved gradually and serendipitously.

The scene in England was transitioning from rock'n'roll to punk. He and his friends, who called themselves *The Weekend Lunatics* were self-taught artists and musicians, not quite hippies and not quite punks.

One day they took a trip together and decided to use the photobooth at the train station. Steve had only used it once before for passport pictures.

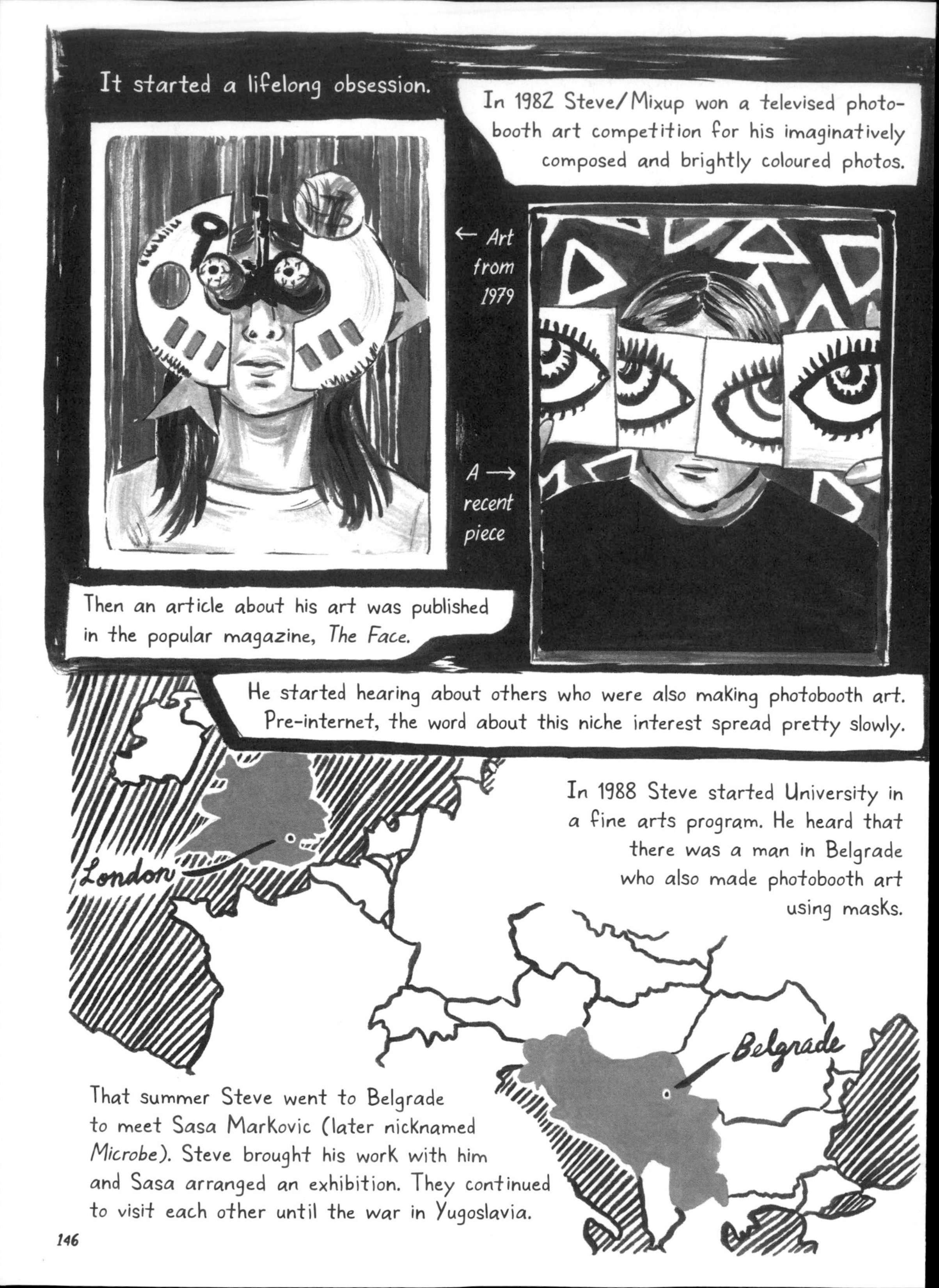

It started a lifelong obsession.
In 1982 Steve/Mixup won a televised photobooth art competition for his imaginatively composed and brightly coloured photos.
← Art from 1979
A → recent piece
Then an article about his art was published in the popular magazine, *The Face.*
He started hearing about others who were also making photobooth art. Pre-internet, the word about this niche interest spread pretty slowly.
In 1988 Steve started University in a fine arts program. He heard that there was a man in Belgrade who also made photobooth art using masks.
London
Belgrade
That summer Steve went to Belgrade to meet Sasa Markovic (later nicknamed *Microbe*). Steve brought his work with him and Sasa arranged an exhibition. They continued to visit each other until the war in Yugoslavia.

Finally in 1994, Sasa was able to visit England and Steve organized a weekend of workshops and got Photo-Me to sponsor it. The whole thing took place in the Glasgow train station.

Mixup's photobooth art enlarged on a billboard in Glasgow, 1994.

These gatherings were the seeds of the first conventions.

The 2002 convention in Brighton, England.

In 1999, Sasa visited again and Steve invited eleven people from around Europe, this time to Nottingham and the first official convention was born.

Steve continued to organize conventions nearly every year in the UK, in Belgrade, and in New York City until 2005 when Photobooth.net launched and Brian and Tim helped with the planning.

The night before the 2012 convention began, Brian invited the out of town guests to his house in Santa Monica.
What seemed like an excited but normal conversation for the rest of the group
BLEW MY MIND
Besides that one meeting with Jeff to discuss the contest, it was the first time I had ever been with other "photoboothers."
The conversation was on a whole other level, it wasn't just fans chatting to each other, but industry folk and experts with the inside scoop. I couldn't keep track of it all. Fortunately, Kory was there to take notes and photos.

We geeked out over Brian's Model 14 that he built a special shed in his backyard to house. We passed around photobooth books and talked about alternative paper options and about the digital photobooth industry.
TAKE
MINI
POR
PHOTOS
It was the first time I could talk openly about my interest, knowing that I wasn't boring the people I was talking to. I felt numb and tingly, like I had finally met a long lost family.
Many of the people there had seen each other in February at the opening of *Derrière le Rideau/Behind the Curtain*, an esteemed exhibit of photobooth art in Switzerland. I knew of the exhibit but I couldn't make a trip to Europe in the middle of the semester.
Musée de l'Élysée in Lausanne, Switzerland.

The next morning Kory and I helped prep the space for the convention that was starting that evening.
Brian organized an exhibit that was based on *PHOTOMATON: A Contemporary Survey of Photobooth Art*, which had been the first major group show of photobooth art that had taken place in NYC in 1987.
For the 25th anniversary, Brian collected new works from all of the artists who participated in the original show.
Three photobooths were delivered to the convention space: one colour, one B&W and one Model 11 that was in excellent condition but not operational.
Art by well known French graffiti artist, Jef Aérosol, one of the original PHOTOMATON artists.
The booths were free for anyone to use.

As we were setting up, a dance recital the same facility was finishing. Tim invited the little dancers to try out the photobooths.
I watched as one girl posed for her pictures like a pro and then instantly checked the chute for her pictures. She informed me that the booth was broken.
I explained that it just took a few minutes because these were "real" pictures, not digital prints. They lost interest in me as I tried to explain darkroom chemistry.
Photobooths in the United States are mostly in bars so most kids today will never experience them. Though, with the abundance of digital cameras, they all seem to be experts at posing for pictures.
It was a good reminder that almost no one cares or thinks about how photographs are made.

His business came about almost accidently in 2007 when he and Andrea bought their first booth a couple months after their wedding. They made a website and started renting it out. Eventually, the business was good enough that Anthony felt comfortable leaving his day job as an architect to focus solely on photobooths.

Anthony bought several more machines and parts from an arcade and was forced to learn the ins and outs of the mechanics.

They found a market for high quality, artisanal, custom photobooths. Most of their customers are museums, bars and eccentric individuals. In recent years, the demand for digital booths and the relative ease of building and servicing them, has focused a lot of their business in that direction.

Most of my questions for Anthony were about the sustainability of chemical photobooths and the industry. Anthony didn't sugar coat the situation.

If chemical booths disappear altogether, people will be upset at first and they'll be forced to re-evaluate their preferences. Life will go on."

On the last day, Anthony casually said to me, "You should come work for us." My eyes widened and I said, "Yes, yes I will figure out a way to do that."

To wrap up the convention, Brian and Tim conceived and organized a Photobooth Pub Crawl. They rented a huge bus and driver, complete with neon lights and stripper poles for about twenty of us to drive around L.A. and visit bars that had photobooths.

When we pulled up to our first bar, you could see the eye rolls of the bouncer and people hanging around outside. But their expressions quickly switched to confusion when they saw us, a bunch of tourists in photobooth t-shirts deboard instead of the typical bunch of frat boys and sorority girls.

On the bus ride, Evelyn and Jocelyn, two badass technicians from Portland, told me crazy stories they had collected over years of servicing booths. There's nothing they haven't seen. They explained a sort of informal technician's code of honour.
They even have tattoos of the old Auto-Photo logo, which is on serial plates.
PHOTO BOOTH
The booth was out of service at one of the bars. It was owned by the company that Jocelyn works for so she was able to open the door with her key and assess the problem.

Camille and Igor are the owners of *La Joyeuse de la Photographie* in Paris. On the bus, Igor told me that the exhibition, *Derrière le Rideau* was on tour. I had missed it in Switzerland but it was opening soon in Brussels.
How didn't I know this earlier?
is it too late to book a trip to Belgium?
My brain immediately set to work trying to devise a way to get to Europe in the next couple of months.
HOW MUCH MONEY IS IN MY BANK ACCOUNT?
AM I CRAZY?

CHA CHA LOUNGE
LOS ANGELES

MODEL 21
-ACTIVE-

This was where Anatol and Ganna came to live out their lives. I thought about how huge and busy the city was but how it probably felt calm for Anatol, in comparison to the obstacles he faced while he was developing the Photomaton.

Anatol continued to invent new mechanisms and devices. In 1930, he and some British backers formed Multipose Portable Cameras Limited and launched the *Maton.*

The small camera used components similar to the Photomaton. Surprisingly, it wasn't a success.

Maton cameras and their photographs, which resemble photobooth pictures, are incredibly rare.

Anatol was good friends with the very famous cowboy/ entertainer/ commentator Will Rogers.

The Josephos bought a large amount of land in Santa Monica beside Will Rogers' own ranch.

Shirley Temple, another one of their neighbours, was the same age as the Josepho boys, Marco and Roy. They say she was too busy to come out and play though.

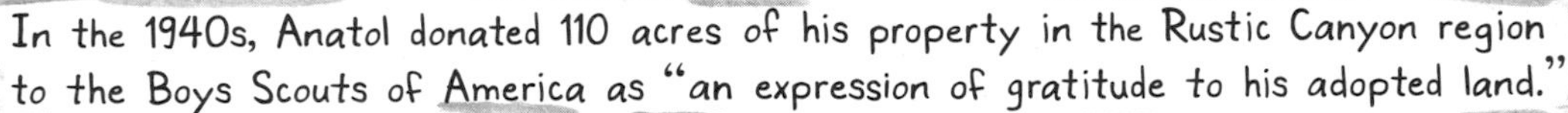

Anatol had a philanthropic nature. He was one of the Founders of the Harry S. Truman Research Institute for the Advancement of Peace, which opened in 1965 in Jerusalem.

Later he was awarded an honorary degree of Doctor of Science and Technology by the Technion in Haifa, Israel.

I went to the convention thinking that I knew a lot about photobooths, which I did compared to most people. But, the convention made it apparent that my knowledge barely scratched the surface of the subject.

MONTREAL

22

For years, while I waited for my pictures to develop, I studied the sample photostrips on the sides of the booths. It didn't take long to notice the recurring faces. I could tell that these weren't copies but original photostrips adhered to the poster and framed behind plexiglass.

PHOT

4 photos 3 minutes $4.00

Gradually, I started unconsciously giving names to all of the Auto-Photo regulars and would wonder who I'd see whenever I approached a booth for the first time.

One person in particular stood out to me, he was on nearly every booth. I started taking photos of his pictures. I named him *Desmond.*

By early 2011, I had amassed a small collection of Desmond sightings, I assumed he was an employee of Auto-Photo. I wrote a blogpost with my findings titled:

A year later, I was contacted by a journalist from CBC Radio, Julia Caron, who read my blog and was curious about my findings.

A photobooth lover herself, Julia interviewed me about my collection, my art projects, and these recurring faces that I had been documenting.

Julia also interviewed the Vice-President of Auto-Photo Canada, Jeff Grostern and she produced a great piece. The radio documentary aired nation-wide several times in the spring of 2012.

I received messages from friends and strangers who had heard the story on the radio and had visited my blog.

Among these was this somewhat cryptic email.

Hi Meags,

I'm Desmond from the Photo-booth, I find your story very interesting. I've actually been on these booths for the last 25 years!

Thanks
Brian, "Desmond"

After the convention, I flew to Montreal primarily to visit Auto-Photo Canada's warehouse. But I also knew that this was my chance to meet the man in the pictures. Brian wasn't an employee of Auto-Photo like I had assumed, his mother had been the receptionist there since he was young.

Brian led us to a Model 17C. We crammed into the booth and prepared for our four snapshots. This was something we had in common, we had both posed for thousands of pictures. Now, the interview could start.

M *How long has your mother worked for Auto-Photo? What's her name again?*

B Her name is Louise, she started there at the same time as George Grostern in the late 70s. If she had to work on weekends she'd take me in with her. So, I started posing in the pictures when I was five or six. They had a Curious George stuffed animal I'd hold in the pictures.

And you took photos pretty often?

Yeah, about once a year, usually in the summer. I'd come in and take a few hundred photos with different colour backgrounds. Jeff would go through them and decide which ones were good enough to go on the booths. I'd get to keep a lot, like all the defective ones.

Do you still have them?

No, no, I don't have them anymore. I gave them away. In high school I'd cut up the strips and write my number on the back and give them to girls.

Haha, they were like business cards. Did it make you popular?

Oh yeah, in high school I'd get recognized all the time. People would say, 'Hey, you're the guy from the photobooth!'

And when I'd go into Auto-Photo, I'd bring my friends too. It was cool because we knew which booths we were on around the city.

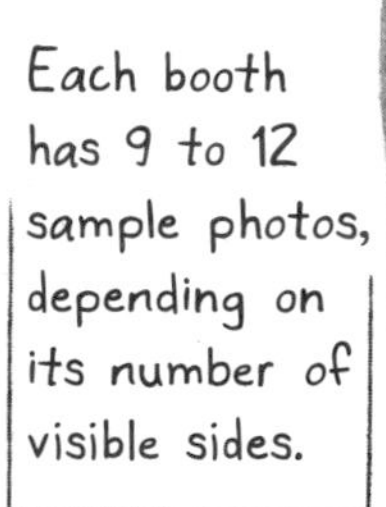

Brian graduated high school in 1998,

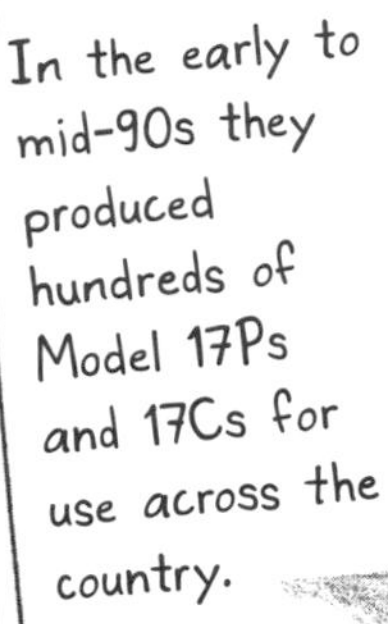

which meant he was featured during a peak time in Auto-Photo's business.

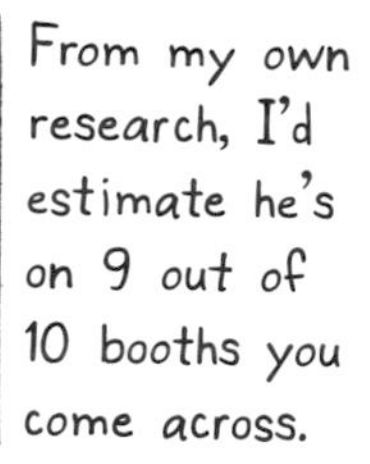

Do you look for yourself when you pass a photobooth now?

Oh yeah, all the time, especially in shopping malls. I feel like a superstar until I walk away.

When was the last time you posed for Auto-Photo?

2005. I can always tell the year by my hairstyle. I posed for them for almost twenty years.

So they inadvertently documented your adolescence. It's funny that photobooths ended up being like time capsules for you. The impact is pretty vast when you think about twenty years of your life being displayed across the country. Do you feel sad about the photobooths disappearing?

No. Well, maybe a little bit. But you have to grow out of it some time.

The CBC documentary broke down that wall and I called Jeff Grostern, who in addition to being the Vice President, is also the grandson of the founder, Samuel Grostern.

After the CBC Radio program aired, I felt comfortable contacting Auto-Photo for the first time. For years, I thought about calling them but the warehouse seemed mythical, like a place I would never be able to visit.

I asked him if I could visit the warehouse and interview him. When he said yes, I felt confident enough to ask for something that I'd dreamed about for a longtime: to have unlimited use of a photobooth for a full day.

JEFF AGREED!

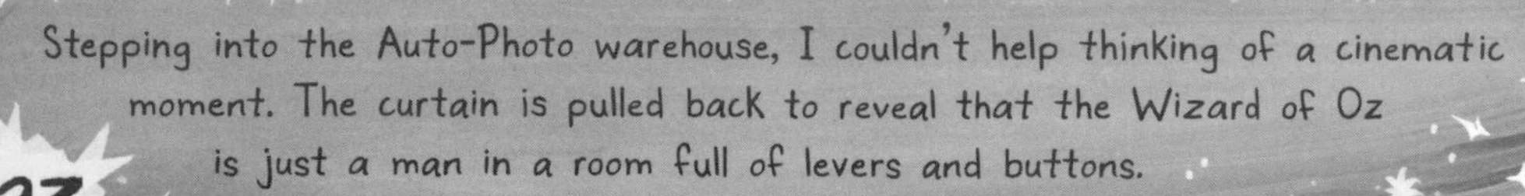

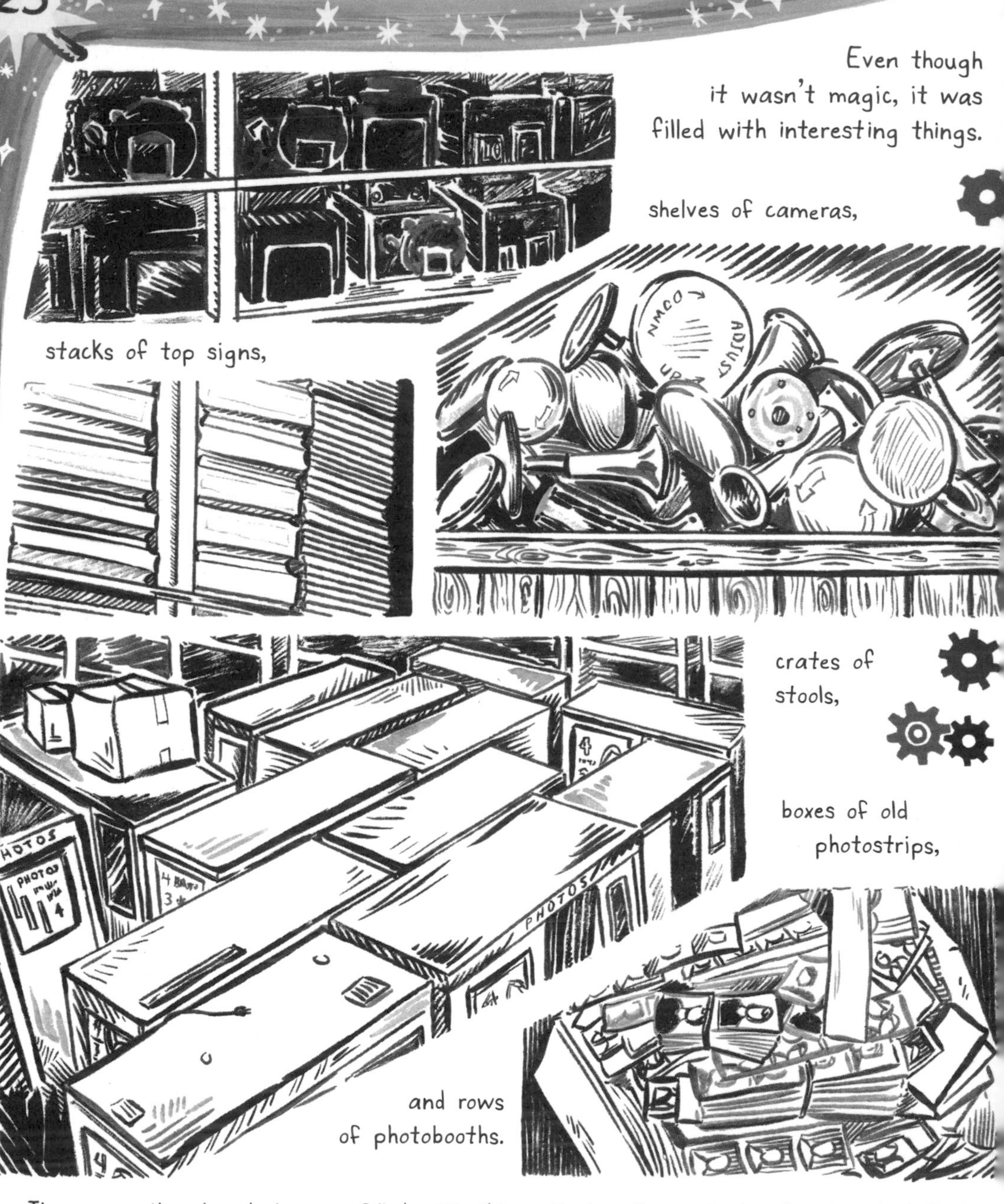

The space, though orderly, was filled with things that no longer had a function but that someone was sentimental enough to keep. I could see that the company has history.

1950 Samuel Grostern, a Montreal businessman and clothing manufacturer went to a convention in NYC.

He witnessed the popularity of Auto-Photo's brand new Model 9. He knew a good thing when he saw it and bought up the Canadian distribution rights.

Without a background in photography or in vending machines, Samuel and his family slowly built up a Canada-wide business.

1976 Samuel's son George, an accountant, bought the business and they introduced colour machines. George is still the President.

1993 George's son Jeff, also an accountant came on as Vice-President and computerized the business.

Over the years they've operated Models 9, 11, 14, 17, 22, which are all the strip-of-four format, but they've had other models too.

Model 41s (B&W) and 24s (colour) have the option of 4 different poses, 4 of the same or 1 large photo. →

The Model 18s make a wider strip of 3 B&W photos. →

Today they only operate colour booths that use the New Processor system. They've taken their B&W dip'n'dunk booths out of circulation.

I instantly liked Jeff. He wasn't a cheesy businessman or so serious that he wouldn't welcome a young artist.

I earned his respect with how much knowledge I had gleaned from just observing trends and tracking serial and model numbers.

On my first day there I shot the photos I needed for a stop motion animation, *Tauro Tauro.* They had a booth with fresh chemicals for me to use.

The booth had a poster on it for an event that had happened on April 26th. I mentioned casually that that date is my birthday. Surprised, Jeff responded that it's also his birthday, *and* his wife's birthday too!

The coincidence was extra strange because the animation was inspired by my relationship with someone whose birthday is *also* April 26th. The stars seemed to be literally aligning.

The next day I returned to interview Jeff and some employees, who were all incredibly friendly and helpful and should be given an award for the nicest staff in Canada. Their loyal team has included individuals who worked there for over forty years before retiring.

Digital booths cost $5, chemical booths cost $4, but they produce the same amount of revenue, which means that when Canadians are given the choice, they are still choosing chemical over digital.

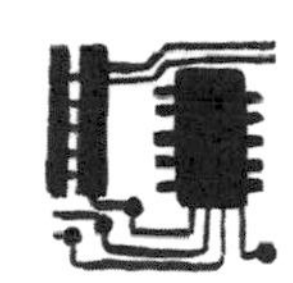

The colour chemical booths have stuck around this long because Auto-Photo is using up a stockpile of colour paper. It used to be produced by Photo-Me Int., but they ceased production in 2007.

Once the reserve is gone the booths will be removed and disposed. The stockpile is anticipated to run out around the summer of 2015.

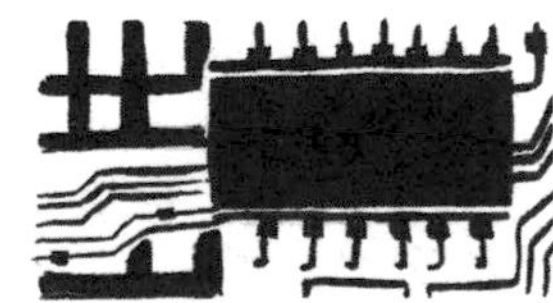

Jeff is practical, he isn't sentimental about his job, despite all his childhood memories of growing up with the company. Business is business.

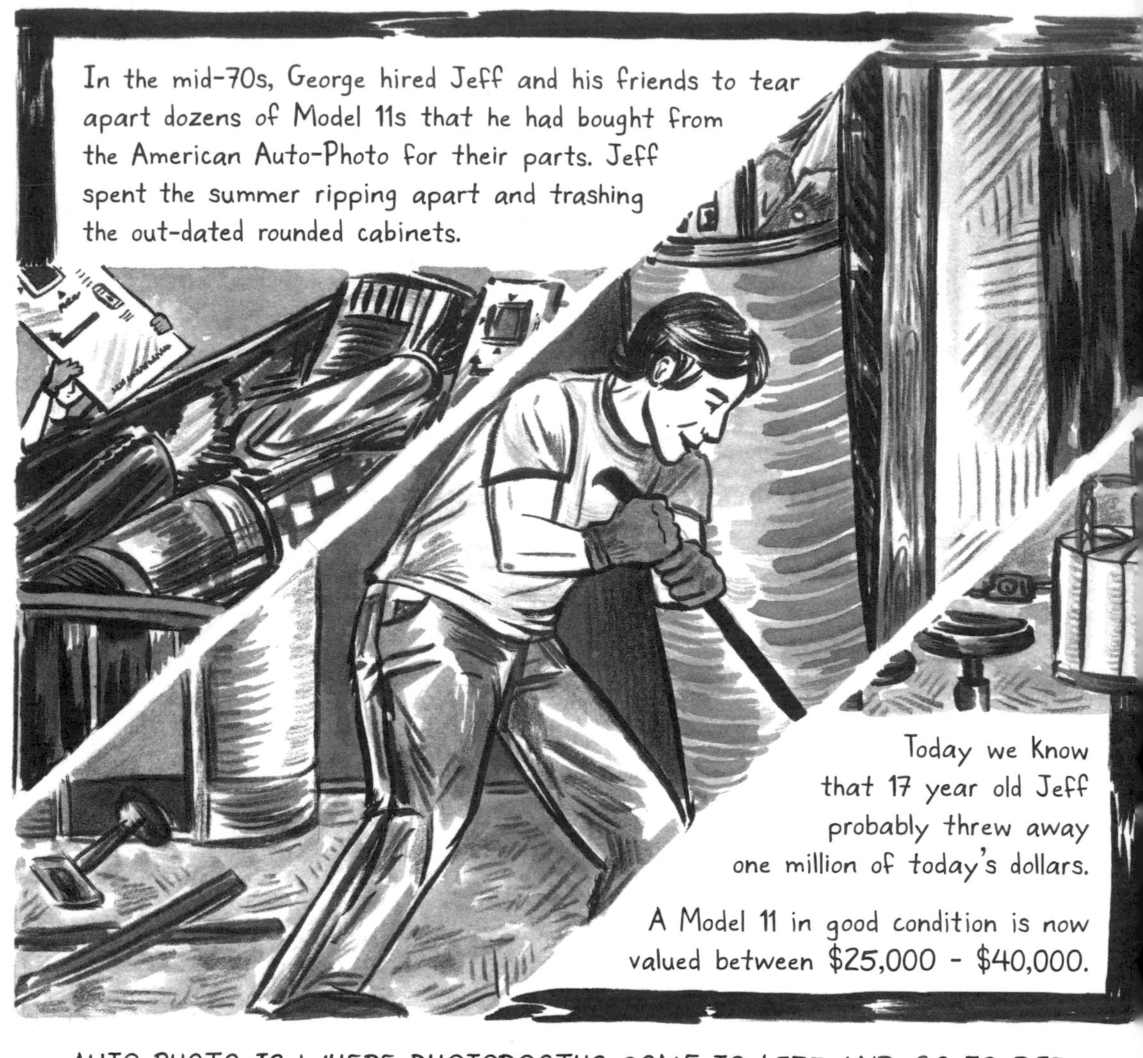

AUTO-PHOTO IS WHERE PHOTOBOOTHS COME TO LIFE AND GO TO DIE. GOING THROUGH THE WAREHOUSE, I FELT BOTH OVERJOYED AND DEEPLY SADDENED.

In forty years, will we look back and kick ourselves for trashing all these photobooths today?

While in Montreal, I was staying with my sister, Eryn. That night we were planning on watching a movie and eating a tub of ice cream.
But when I got back from Auto-Photo, I was overflowing with conflicting emotions.
Jeff told me that they got rid of over half the booths in the Montreal Metro system in the winter of 2012, from 40 to 22 booths.
This included the last two working Model 24s.
These weren't just numbers to me. These were booths I knew well, that I had formed relationships with. I had made trips to Montreal just to use those Model 24s.
Taken at bus station on March 10, 2010.
Eryn tried to subdue my feelings.
This is just par for the course, old technology is always replaced by new technology. What did you expect to happen?
Neither Eryn nor the ice cream could make me feel better.

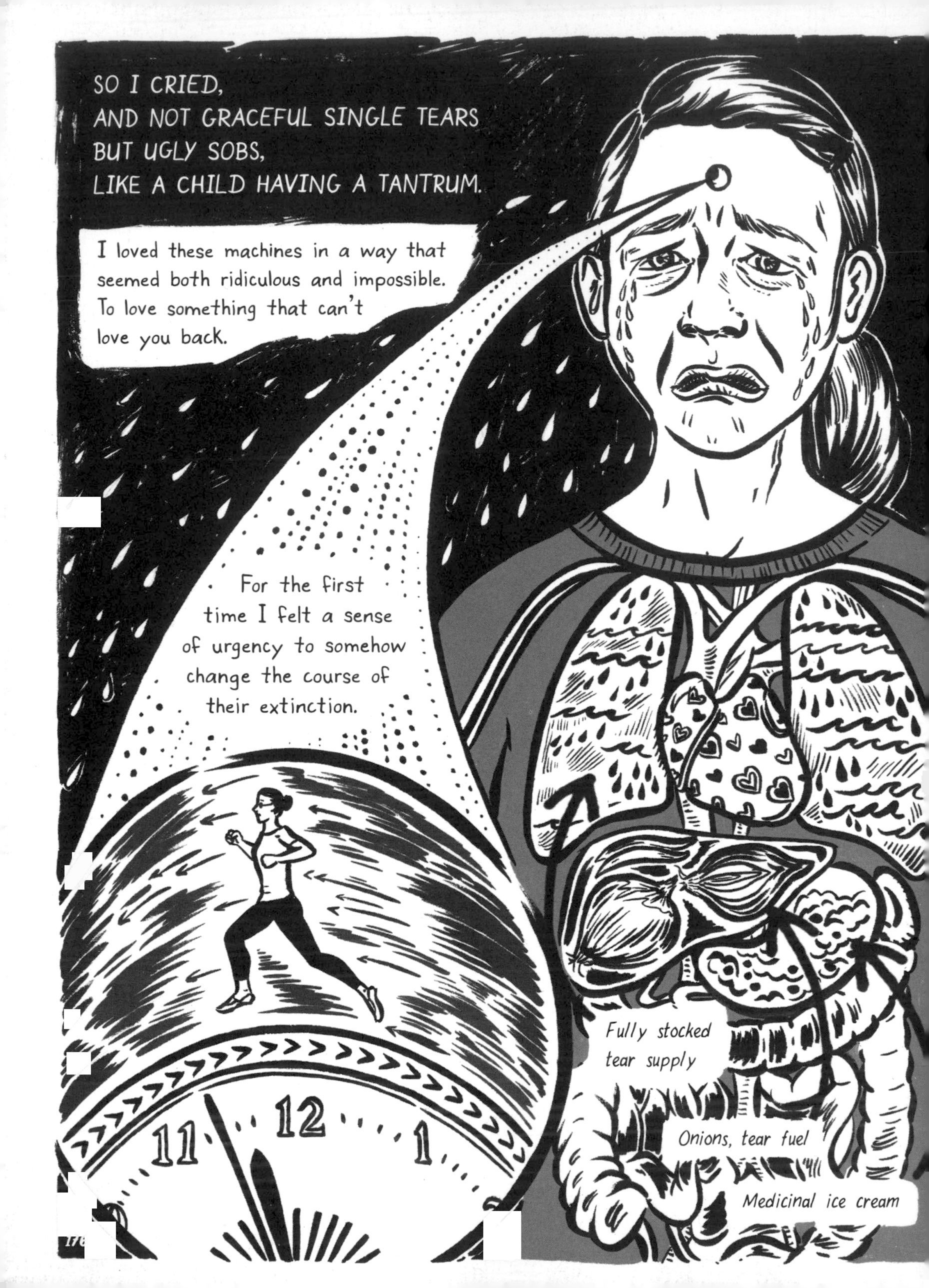
SO I CRIED,
AND NOT GRACEFUL SINGLE TEARS
BUT UGLY SOBS,
LIKE A CHILD HAVING A TANTRUM.
I loved these machines in a way that seemed both ridiculous and impossible. To love something that can't love you back.
For the first time I felt a sense of urgency to somehow change the course of their extinction.
Fully stocked tear supply
Onions, tear fuel
Medicinal ice cream
11
12
1

1 PORTRAIT
4 IDENTIQUES IDENTICAL
4 DIFFERENTES DIFFERENT FLASH
STM
PHOTOS
4 IDENTIQUES IDENTICAL
1 PORTRAIT
4 DIFFERENTES DIFFERENT
3 minutes
$4.
PLACE DES ARTS
METRO
montreal
extinct

24
Back in Halifax, I had a dilemma. I didn't have all the money I needed to go to Brussels, but I did have the time.
I knew that in recent years Auto-Photo had found a market for their old dip'n'dunk machines in Europe. Entrepreneurs were buying them up and I was curious to see this new scene in person.
EUROPE
AMSTERDAM
BRUSSELS
PARIS
NÎMES
TURIN
MILAN
FLORENCE
I reasoned that I could always make more money but I couldn't ever go back in time to see this art exhibit.
So, I contacted photo-booth experts across Europe and mapped out a trip.
Under all the excitement, I was sad to miss the summer in Halifax. I wasn't going to see my friends and I had to end things with someone I'd been dating.
My amazing friends:
Lindsay
Mike
Krista
Nathan
Hank, a fat cat that I had on loan for a year that I had to return early.
I booked my flights, bought a Eurorail pass, and packed my bags.
>>>>>>>>>>>>

In the early morning I was greeted by a downpour.

This was my first time visiting the city and the flip flopping between French and Dutch made navigating disorienting.

At least I had packed light.

The jetlag dampened my general perspective.

WHO DO I THINK I AM?
I CAN'T JUST FLY TO ANOTHER CONTINENT AND SPEND THOUSANDS OF DOLLARS TO SEE AN ART SHOW!

Then I took a nap and everything was fine.

I spent seven hours looking over all the pieces multiple times, making observations and taking notes. I eavesdropped on other attendees, listening for their thoughts and writing them down.

Excerpt from my journal:

The most successful pieces are unbelieveable and defy photobooth logic (like Jan Wenzel) or are utterly simple (like Naomi Leibowitz.) The pieces by the show's big names, Andy Warhol and Cindy Sherman don't hold up beside the lesser known artists, who are more familiar with the photobooth as a tool & medium.

One of the themes of the show was *A Deux C'est Mieux.** It featured decades worth of found photos of couples, some darling and innocent, others vulgar and x-rated.

It's been well recorded that the tight and private booths invite couples in

and the photo-taking spurs on spontaneous acts. Photo-booths have earned their naughty reputation.

But the *A Deux C'est Mieux* theme struck a personal chord and stung.

I had just chosen to miss a summer with my friends and I didn't have the kind of support that Kory and Eryn offered in Los Angeles and Montreal.

*Une Suffit*** doesn't have the same ring to it.

* approximate translation: *Together is Better*

** translation: *One Will Do*

Some highlights were Michel Folco's album of found photos, Tomoko Sawada's hundreds of self-portraits under different identities, Hansjürg Buchmeier's video *Very Last Pictures*, and the original photographs of the Surrealists playing in photobooths.

Something about this photo of the French poet, Paul Éluard resonated with me.

By closing his eyes, he is saying *the camera sees me but I don't see the camera.* Thereby removing his concern of how he appears in photographs.
This gave me a sense of relief.

At the gallery, *La Joyeuse de Photographie*, Igor & Camille's company, had a booth in the lobby.

It was installed for the exhibit, but as the only chemical booth in Brussels, it was doing very well and so the gallery decided to keep it there long-term.

I used the booth, borrowing Éluard's closed eyes and posing with the exhibition catalogue. (I grew up speaking French, so I could mostly read it.)

← *Sculpture by Constantin Meunier in the courtyard of Le Botanique.*

PHOTOS
Photos
Photos
LE BOTANIQUE BRUSSELS -active-

25
I spent a few more days in Belgium, and then headed to Paris. There I was greeted by my dear friend Marion, who I had stayed with in 2009.
Marion and I might as well be twins separated at birth. I don't know anyone else more like myself.
Any loneliness I was feeling quickly quelled with her company.
CAFÉ
My visit was timed perfectly, Marion was on a break between semesters so she had time to help me track down and visit photobooths across Paris.
MERLO
Figue
Rhubarbe
PARIS PRATIQUE
PARIS PRATIQUE
← Cheap wine and yogurt flavours that you can't get in Canada.

Marion's help was indispensable. Her ability to navigate the city and her far superior communication skills made our photobooth hunt very efficient.

We spent three straight days going to locations that I had tips for.

Often we'd arrive at a location to discover the booth had been moved. Like detectives we questioned staff for leads as to its new whereabouts.

We passed an amusement park and I saw that there was a *Train Fantome*. I begged Marion to ride it with me.

In a scene in *Amélie*, she goes on the ride hoping to return Nino's lost album of photobooth pictures. Nino is employed as a skeleton and fondles Amélie's neck.

A masked skeleton surprised us too, but it was much less sexy.

On our third day of photobooth hunting, my eyes locked on a huge mural facing the courtyard of the Centre Pompidou. I recognized the style right away.

It was made by Jef Aérosol, the French artist who participated in the 1987 *Photomaton* exhibition and in the 25 Year Anniversary show at the convention. I could only interpret this as a very good omen.

When Marion was with me we took fun photos, but when I was by myself, I closed my eyes.

It relieved the pressure I felt to pose.

It wasn't about the picture, it was about the hunt and the experience. The picture is just an artifact that says: "I was here."

FORUM DES IMAGES PARIS

Camille and I met on a patio where she and Igor had a photobooth placed for the summer.

We talked about the many differences between the Canadian and French chemical photobooth scenes. Chemical booths disappeared entirely in France for a few years when the switch to digital was made.

La Joyeuse de la Photographie bought most of their booths from Auto-Photo Canada.

France loves its photobooths and the people know the difference between chemical and digital, they're excited to use vintage booths.

I was seriously impressed when she told me how much revenue their booths generate, particularly the very well located ones.

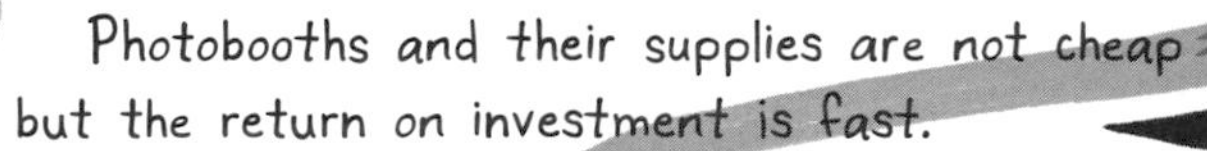

Photobooths and their supplies are not cheap but the return on investment is fast.

The grassroots movement isn't giving new life to old machines just for nostalgic purposes, it's a very profitable business model. In recent years, many small companies have sprung up across Europe and elsewhere with similar business plans.

This has significantly contributed to the upswing of photobooths but I wonder how sustainable it is, given the looming potassium dichromate ban and the gradual depletion of materials and machine parts.

I contacted a few other individuals who've started small businesses.

IMOGEN IN IRELAND

Imogen is an artist living in Dublin. She remembers taking I.D. photos in a photobooth as a child. As an adult she began collecting cameras and thought it would be wonderful to own a photobooth, like one giant camera to add to her collection. In 2010 she bought one and had it shipped overseas from Chicago.

She calls it the *Photo Robot* and keeps it in a bar in Dublin, though it gets moved around a fair bit to festivals and events.

Imogen's been running it as a successful side business and is currently the only person operating a chemical photobooth in all of Ireland. It's her labour of love and in turn, it's much loved by her community.

PAULA IN AUSTRALIA

Paula has been collecting photostrips of herself since 1992 and has plans to document her whole life this way. When she noticed that booths were disappearing, she decided to buy one to keep the act of documentation going. A friend of Paula's asked her if she could use it at her wedding and a rental business was born.

Paula is one of a few people in Australia who operates a vintage photobooth rental service. *Strip Of A Lifetime* is located in Newcastle.

Paula also has a storefront which contains an Analog Art Gallery and other vintage trinkets. She now runs her business with her husband, Nathan. They met when he was managing a music venue and was seeking a photobooth for the space. Their whole courtship has been documented in their Model 17.

RAFAEL IN ENGLAND AND SPAIN

Rafael is a professor living in London who has a love of photography. He got the idea of buying a chemical photobooth to use at his close friend's wedding. But the booth was delivered late and his original vision was not possible. When it did finally arrive he had a big, heavy and delicate machine to figure out.

Eventually, under the name *The Original Photobooth*, Rafael got two booths up and running in venues in London.

Now he's in the process of re-introducing chemical photo-booths in Spain. Under the name *Photomaticon* he has a booth in Barcelona and several more locations planned.

His business is driven by his passion for keeping the photo machine alive.

Language barriers made it difficult for me to connect with everyone I would have liked to talk to about their businesses. I recognized that my survey of the contemporary scene and even my knowledge of the history, though accurate, was likely omitting developments outside of the Western world.

Decades ago, chemical photobooth companies were very active in South America, South Asia and in some African countries, which made me wonder if any sort of revival movement has sprung up in those areas as well.

A country's economic condition would play a large factor in the viability of an indie business. But economics aside, I feel confident that people all over could feel nostalgic for vintage photobooths.

While I was still in Belgium, I had made a day trip to Bruges. The town was built at the end of the medieval era and is now packed with tourists.

It's been so well maintained that it sometimes appears to be staged.

Visiting the little town inspired some questions.

Excerpts from my journal:

When does something transition from just being old to being an antique? Or from out-of-style to vintage?

HOW OLD DOES SOMETHING NEED TO BE BEFORE ITS INITIAL VALUE IS RESTORED? AND THEN HOW MUCH LONGER UNTIL THAT VALUE IS SURPASSED?

How common is it that something's initial value will ever be earned back? What are the odds that it will just become garbage?

I walked through a flea market and saw old things everywhere that were assigned new values, some seemed too low and others too high. The time it takes (or doesn't take) for an object's worth to increase varies with so many factors.

HOW ACCURATE OF AN ASSESSMENT CAN I MAKE NOW OF WHERE PHOTOBOOTHS FALL ON THIS SPECTRUM?

FROM BRUGES TO PARIS,
I WAS REMINDED THAT THE FUTURE IS ALREADY HERE.

In a mall in Paris, my eye was caught by the most futuristic digital photobooth I've ever seen.

The seat was orange and semi-transparent. It illuminated from the inside, the light pulsed and drew me to it. Despite my aversion to digital booths, I inserted euros.

I found out later that Photo-Me International hired the famous designer StARCK to design them a booth. It's certainly simple and clean and kinda sexy.

StARCK saw the seat as the heart of the booth, so it pulses at the rate of a heartbeat.

In my journal I wrote:

HOW ARE VINTAGE BOOTHS SUPPOSED TO COMPETE WITH THIS?

Unlike other digital booths, this photo-taking experience wasn't trying to replicate a chemical booth, it was its own unique experience.

LES HALLES, PARIS
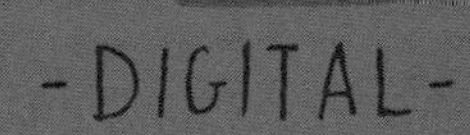
-DIGITAL-

I had a meeting with Marc Bellini, an artist and teacher at the esteemed École Nationale Supérieure des Beaux-Arts.
I was already familiar with Marc's work and curious about his academic approach to making art. He travels to North America once a year to use a colour photobooth and execute several projects all at once.
His works are inspired by philosophy and art history, they're meticulously planned and he rehearses his poses endlessly to perfect his timing.
It's appropriate that he calls photobooths the "Little Theatres of the Self."
I could tell that Marc sees the world through a specific lens and that his work fits in to a high art world, which is an interesting juxtaposition for the common photobooth.

I had one big reason for my trip to Paris and it made me very nervous.

One of the curators of *Derrière le Rideau*, Clément Chéroux agreed to let me interview him for one hour in his office at the Centre Georges Pompidou.

The largest museum for modern art in Europe.

I was nervous because in art school the hierarchy of institutional art was engrained in us. Curators are near the top, especially curators who work for prestigious museums. Somehow, I, some artsy kid from Canada, cheated the system and got an hour of this man's time.

Clément is also a historian of photography and he is clearly driven by a love for the subject. I could tell right away that he wasn't just someone capitalizing on the novelty of photobooths but that he was a genuine photobooth fan.

It was invigorating to talk to someone who had clearly thought about photobooths on every level and who has a personal connection to them.
For me the photobooth is a kind of sculpture, a monument, a temple to photography.
It feels mystical.
Clément's been collecting material on the subject for more than twenty years.
I learned that he and the other curators only included about 20% of the photo-booth art that they found in the final exhibition.
The number gave me perspective of how many artists are actually working with this medium.
Their vision behind Derrière le Rideau was to find artists who were saying something about photobooths, not just playing in them.

Clément introduced me to the idea that photobooths are like uteruses and I had a personal revelation. In art school, my work was about spaces that served as surrogate wombs. I realized back then that I had a pattern of seeking that in-utero feeling.
Somehow, I hadn't made the connection earlier. The enclosure of a photobooth is a womb-like space and I had been finding comfort in it for so long.
I asked him about photo-booths as time machines.
I told him that I had found many people who could romanticize the past, but hadn't found anyone yet who could romanticize the future of photobooths.
Clément believes that they operate as a form of cultural time machine but that they can only go backwards. In the future, there is only a void.
I felt affirmed after the interview. My project wasn't crazy, or if it was, at least there were other crazy people out there too.

From the Pompidou, I decided to visit Père Lachaise, the cemetery where many famous figures are buried.

I had been there years earlier and had wandered the labyrinth of tombstones and mausoleums. This time I went to visit someone specific.

Paul Éluard has a simple and understated grave, not far from Oscar Wilde's monument, covered in lipstick kisses. In comparison, Éluard's grave gives the impression that he doesn't have too many visitors.

It made me think that if technicians are the brains of the photobooth, artists must be the souls.

I was sad to say goodbye to Marion, but it had been a great and productive visit.

The purpose of my trip was to visit one of the world's largest private collections of working vintage arcade games in a small town outside of Amsterdam.

We couldn't have prepared for the wonder of their home and collection, all of which pays homage to America in the 1950s.

Peter and Ina have been collecting vintage jukeboxes and arcade machines for over thirty years and bought the house they live in now to hold their sizable collection. They also dress the part, wearing clothes authentic to the era.

The basement is dedicated to their main collection. Every item has been expertly restored to working order. The space feels like a museum, with special lighting and murals, but it also has a levity that invites you to play and enjoy the snack bar.

For over a decade Ina coveted a Model 11 in a nearby vintage shop but it was priced at 6,000 euros. When the shop closed, Peter was able to buy the booth for a deal and surprise Ina with it as a Christmas gift.

The booth is in pristine condition. They didn't want the chemicals in their home, so they had it converted to take and print digital photos without effecting any original parts.

I was in awe of the condition and completeness of their collection. It's so much more than an interest or hobby, they are living amongst their passion.

Afterwards, Ina drove Cari and I to the nearest metro stop and I asked her if they visit the USA often. She told me that they've never been. Peter doesn't like flying and they aren't very interested in present day America.

I had a lead on a photobooth warehouse in Holland, about three hours away on the bus. I called them on Friday and left a voice message. I didn't hear anything back over the weekend so I planned to leave on Monday.

But early Monday morning, I was woken by a call saying that I could visit. I had a quick decision to make.

DO I FOLLOW MY ITINERARY AND LEAVE THE NETHERLANDS?

OR

DO I THROW OUT MY PLANS AND TAKE A CHANCE ON THIS WAREHOUSE WHICH SWITCHED TO DIGITAL YEARS AGO?

WAIT 10 MINUTES

TRANSFER

I embraced my sense of adventure, Cari scribbled some dizzying directions down for me, and I was on my way.

WALK 5 BLOCKS SOUTH

THE MOMENT I WALKED IN, I KNEW I HAD MADE THE RIGHT DECISION.

In the doorway was a very rare booth made by the Zurich ProntoPhot Company in the early 60s.

← Hydraulic seat

↖ Coin receptors and selection panel

I arrived there minutes before closing but Peter, the service manager who was about to go home and start his summer vacation, could see my enthusiasm and offered to stay late. He told me that I was the first writer to visit them and I felt like an anthropologist uncovering a lost treasure.

ProntoPhot was bought by Photo-Me International in 1998 and switched their machines to digital in 2004. Peter's worked there for almost thirty years.

Prontophot

Sample photos from their brochure from the 60s.

It wasn't company policy but he always kept one of each booth model before scrapping the rest.

So the warehouse serves as an archive of historical European photobooths.

Model 11 door with Dutch text

I saw several different ProntoPhot models that were made before their merger with Photo-Me. All their booths produced photos in a square sheet rather than a strip.

Model for shopping malls.

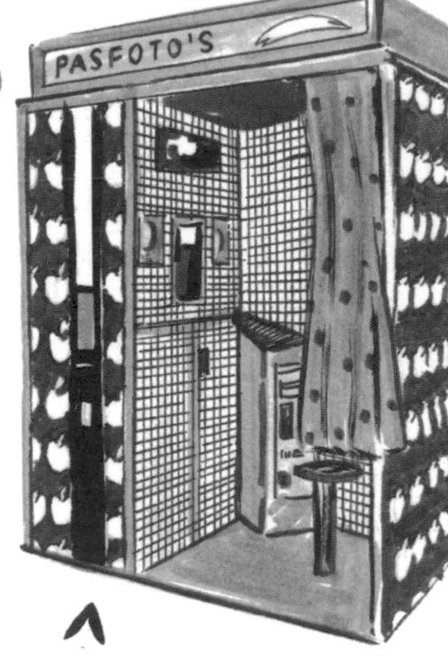

Apple siding and gingham interior.

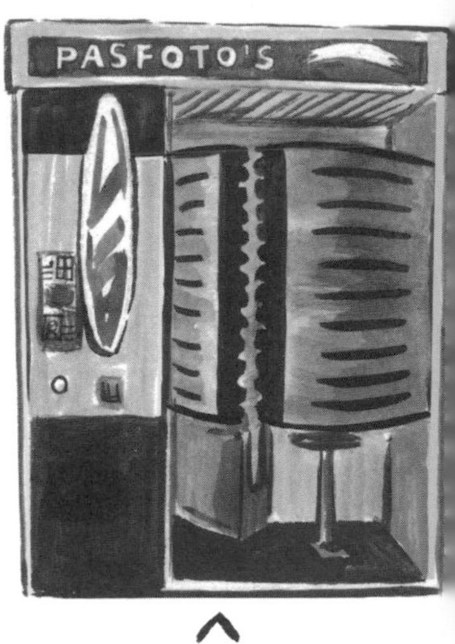

Curtainless for train stations.

Coin receptor is made of steel and is separate from photo processing area as an anti-theft measure.

I appreciated the time Peter spent with me but even more I appreciated his passion for his work and its history. Without people like him, this type of information gets lost.

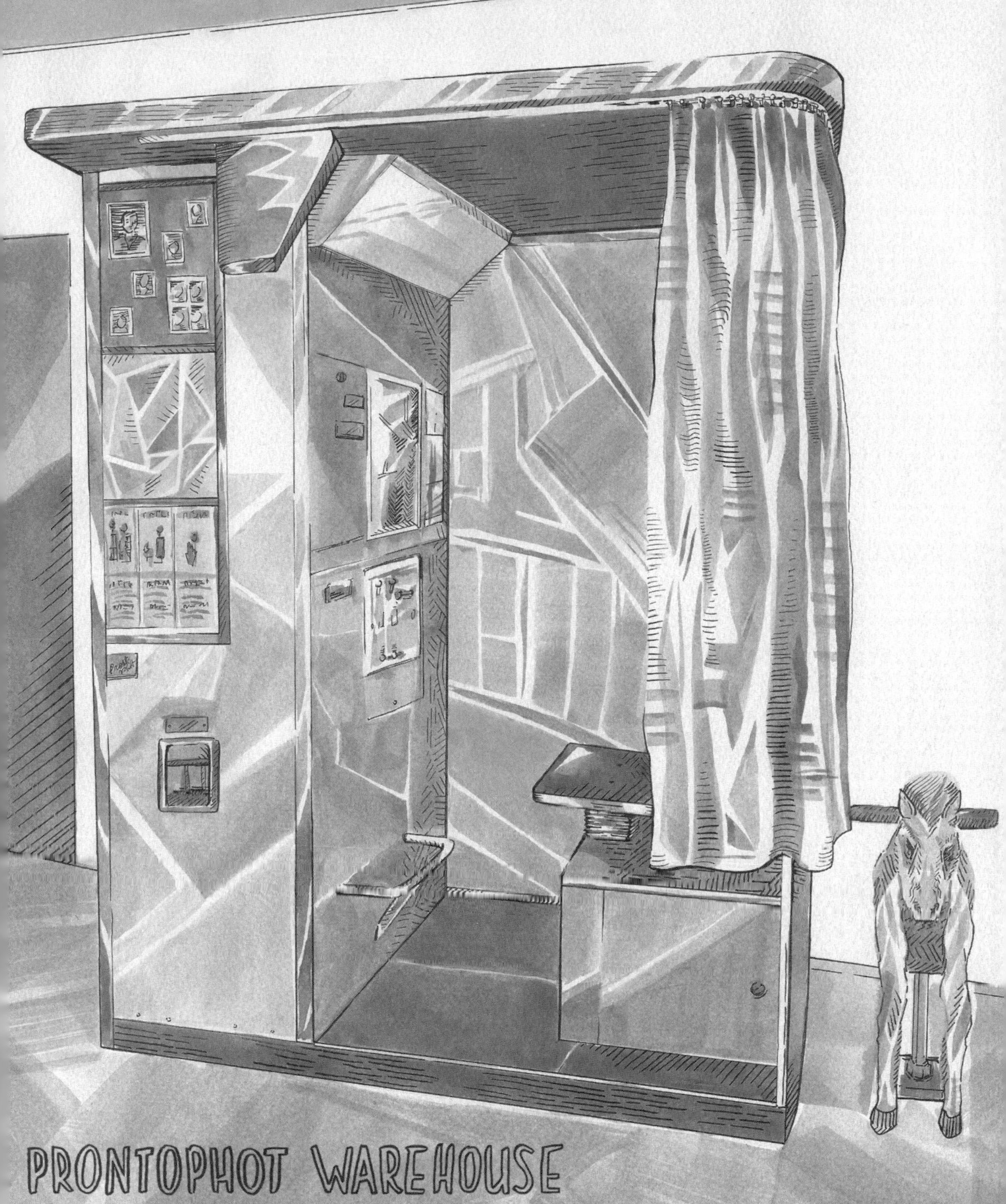

PRONTOPHOT WAREHOUSE
HAPERT, HOLLAND

PRONTOPHOT ZURICH MODELL 9

--INACTIVE--

My next stop was the South of France. However, I had some trouble when I tried to use my Eurorail pass. When I had travelled in Europe in 2009, it was winter and I didn't have to make reservations in addition to having the pass.

It just didn't occur to me that in the summer I would need to reserve my seats far in advance.

So, instead of direct routes, I had to travel by making many connections from one small train to another.

After much ado, I arrived in beautiful Nîmes. I was there to meet and stay with Les Matons, an artist couple who've been making art with photobooths since 1988.

Built during the Roman Empire.

Les Matons are Christian and Hélène, their art is unlike anything else I've seen. They don't differentiate between chemical and digital booths. Their work is conceptual yet very accessible.

They use booths as 'instant art-making machines' and enjoy the inexactness of it all.

They don't take it too seriously and there's a liveliness in their work that I don't often see.

In the 90s, a cinema hired them to make some promotions. Les Matons made photobooth art interpreting classic films which were then blown up on billboards.

They've made two books of photobooth art which focus more on the relationship between the images than effects and camera tricks.

Their art is just like their apartment, filled with little wonders in every nook and cranny.

From Nîmes I took a day trip to the nearby town of Arles to see *Les Rencontres d'Arles Photographie.* I went to see a special B&W photobooth that Fotoautomat France made for the event.

The booth was ultra stylish with a space age inspired design.

I used it and then sat in the sun and observed other people as they interacted with it. Everyone was laughing.

The subject of photobooths had become so loaded for me that often I forgot that they are supposed to be simple and fun.

I was about to leave when I noticed a man approaching with jugs of water, sure enough he was the technician.

While walking around Arles I had noticed these 3 x 4 foot photographs plastered on walls in unsuspecting places. Many of them were peeling off or had graffiti tagged over them.

I asked the technician about these strange, large portraits of smiling people.

He told me that they were by the French artist JR, as a project he did for the exhibition in 2011. He's done this project all over the world.

JR built a digital photobooth attached to a huge printer. He invites the public to take their self-portrait and provides the glue and tools to plaster the town with the faces of its citizens.

I love this idea and feel that it makes sense for photobooth art to exist outside of the gallery.

In addition to not reserving my seats in advance, I had made another not-so-smart oversight in my trip planning. I didn't really account for the time it takes to get from one city to another. Compared to Canada, it seemed like all European cities were right next door to each other.

THIS IS NOT ACTUALLY TRUE.

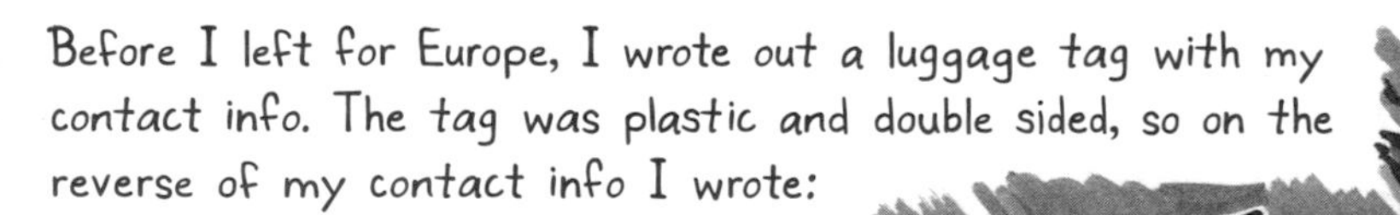

Before I left for Europe, I wrote out a luggage tag with my contact info. The tag was plastic and double sided, so on the reverse of my contact info I wrote:

SEE OTHER SIDE

In Amsterdam, Cari remarked that the luggage tag was like an existential message that I subliminally wrote to myself. Like, I must *see the other side of photobooths* before I could fully understand them. At the time, I chuckled at the idea.

I couldn't get from Nîmes to Florence in one day. Unfortunately, I had to stop in Turin for one night. By the time I realized this, all the hostels in central Turin were booked. I found one place in the outskirts that had one room left. Last check-in was at 10pm.
I had to take three trains to get to Turin, which included going west to Marseilles before I could go east to Ventimiliga. Every train was behind schedule that day and so I kept missing my connections.
My small suitcase was getting heavy. I had been getting rid of clothes along the way in order to fit more books.
I was wheeling around a library of rare photobooth books.
The pull-out handle bumped against the same spots on the backs of my legs as I walked and some tender bruises had been forming.
Everything got much more difficult when I entered Italy. I don't speak any Italian and was hoping to get by communicating in English or French.
I was hot. I was tired. I was aggravated.
«il treno è in ritardo«
«IL PREZZO É DI 15 EURO«
«è necessaria una prenotazione«

Every time I switched trains and had to lift my suitcase out of the racks, my eyes locked on SEE OTHER SIDE. The message felt like it was hitting me in the face... and literally, quite painfully behind my legs.

The message felt like it was coming from a voice inside my head.

I missed my last train by two minutes and had to take a local commuter train instead. It was a six hour ride on essentially a subway.

I would arrive in Turin at 9:30 PM and make it to my hostel in the nick of time.

Fortunately, the train had air conditioning. Unfortunately, it leaked some mystery fluid through cracks in the ceiling panels.

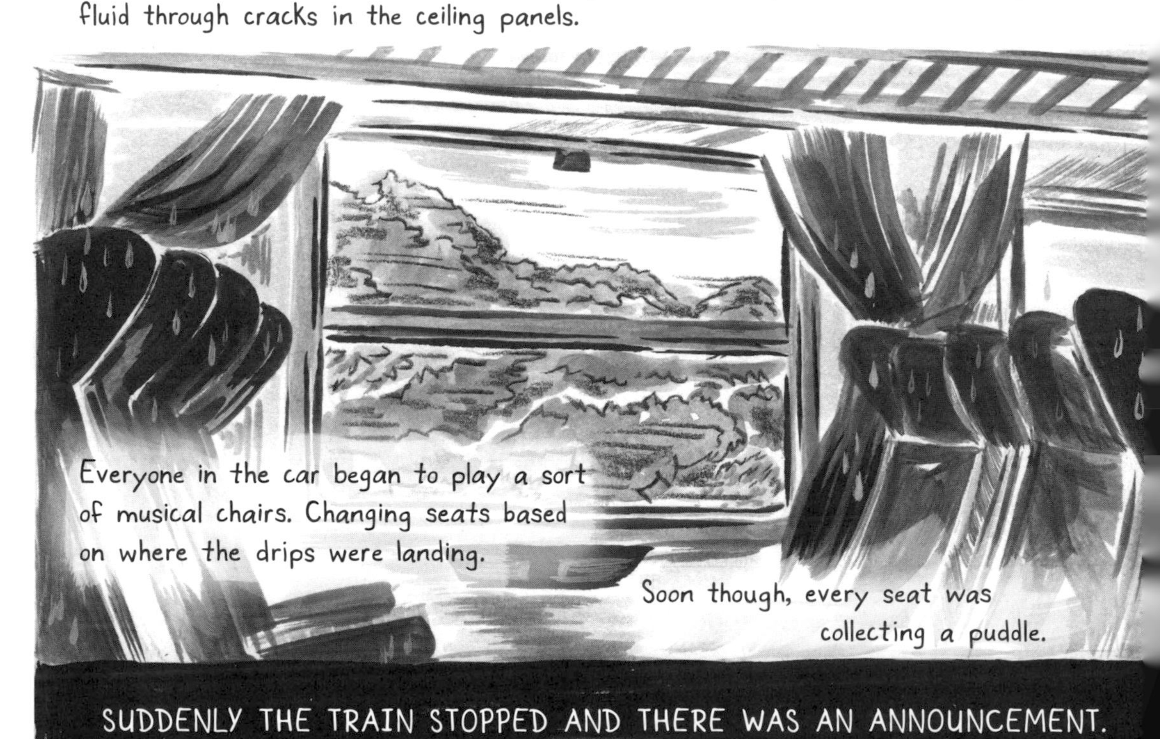

I didn't understand it. The woman sitting across from me looked upset. I asked her to translate.

She hesitated but did her best to explain with basic English.

THE TRAIN I AM ON KILLED SOMEONE.

After a few minutes of wrapping my head around the situation, I remembered that I still needed a place to sleep that night. I made the most expensive phone call of my life and pleaded with the hostel to stay open later so I could check-in. They agreed but only until 11 PM.

The train sat still. The ceiling dripped. I ruminated.

As the wait continued, I grew tired and my thoughts softened. My mind put things into perspective.

I thought of Anatol's long journey back to Russia, just to see his father one more time. He was on trains far worse than this during wartime. He was in real danger, not just in danger of having to sleep in a train station for one night.

What *is* the other side to photobooths? I knew photobooths hadn't always been used as fun keepsakes or for practical I.D. photos.

1952

The new Auto-Photo Company knew photobooths had a market outside of amusement parks. Shortly after their successful debut of the Model 9, they developed the Model 10. It was designed for police stations and jails and were advertised to police personnel who were inexperienced in photography.

Its interior was likely identical to the Model 9 but it operated with the push of a button instead of with coins. The cost of a photostrip, (excluding the price of the booth) worked out to three cents per strip.

1955

Improving on the technology, Auto-Photo made the Model 11A, which was essentially a Model 11 without the chrome details and the colourful accents. Its function was to document government employees and military personnel, as well as take mugshots for criminal records.

Auto-Photo sold booths to prisons across the US for many decades. These mugshots, which are very difficult to find, likely reflect a different America than what we're used to seeing through a photobooth lens.

In May 1940, Germany occupied France. A year later the Société Continentale Photomaton (the French division) issued a letter to the German authorities.

Nous pensons que le rassemblement de certaines catégories d'individus de race juive dans des camps de concentration aura pour consécuence administrative la constitution d'un dossier, d'une fiche ou carte, etc.

Spécialistes des questions ayant trait à l'identité, nous nous permettons d'attirer particulièrement votre attention sur l'intérêt que présentent

Translation:

"We imagine that the assembly of certain categories of individuals of the Jewish race in concentration camps will necessarily result in the administrative need to create dossiers, files and identity cards, etc.

We are specialists in matters concerning identification, and so we venture to bring to your attention in particular how useful our automatic Photomaton machines would be. They are capable of photographing a thousand people in six different poses, in just one routine day of work. In cases where it is necessary to photograph significant numbers of workers, we bring machines, with an operator, out to the site. We have done this when it was necessary to execute identification photographs, in the plant buildings themselves, of the staffs of the leading French factories. We have also undertaken identification photo campaigns in work camps and prison camps."

French military personnel, circa 1940.

The Photomaton Company did not secure a contract for concentration camps.

For documentation, camps assigned prisoners who had been photographers to use a process that required negatives and took three photos side by side.

The number of work and prisoner of war camps the Photomaton Company did service is unknown. For perspective, by 1944, there were 1.1 million forced civilian labourers just in occupied France. No doubt, many chilling photobooth portraits were taken during the war. I can only speculate that they were destroyed or are preserved in an archive somewhere.

TO ME, PHOTOBOOTHS HAVE ALWAYS FELT LIKE SANCTUARIES, BUT FOR SO MANY, THEY MUST HAVE FELT LIKE CASKETS, SEALING THEIR FATE.

The train started moving,

I had four more hours to my destination to think and calm down.

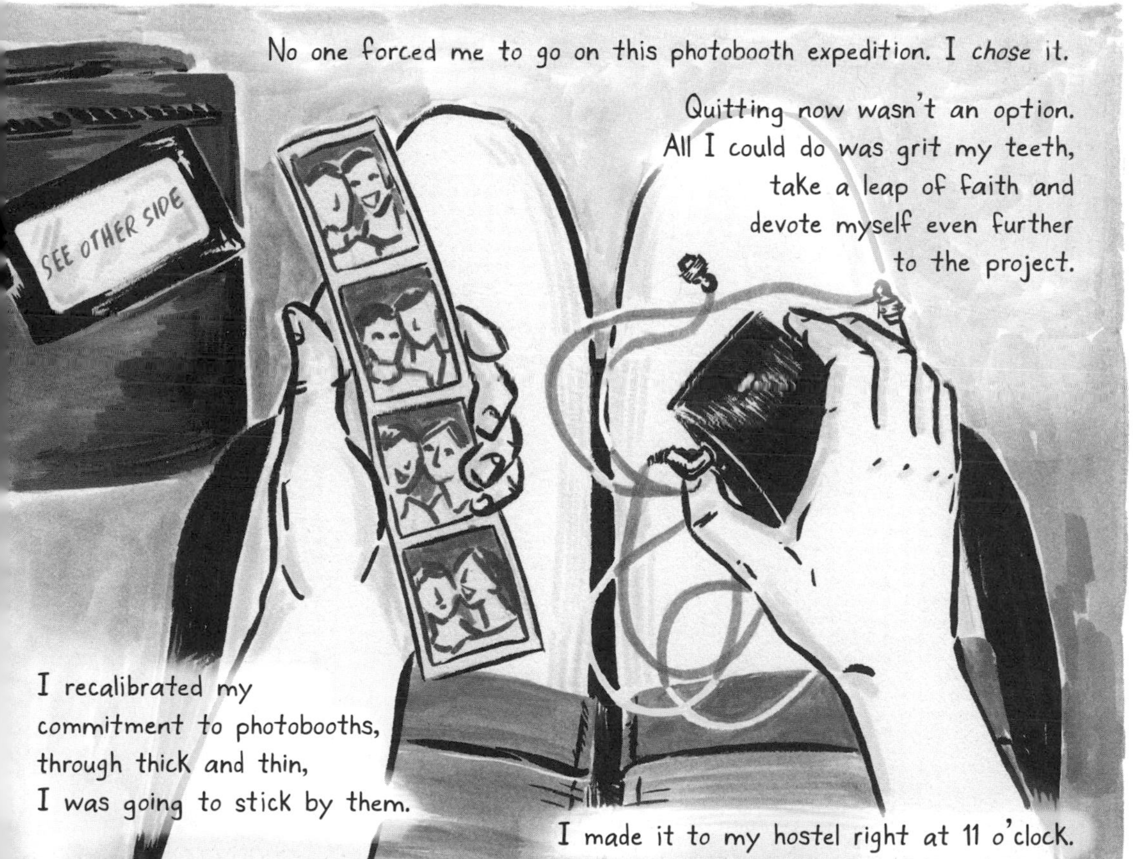

No one forced me to go on this photobooth expedition. I *chose* it.

Quitting now wasn't an option. All I could do was grit my teeth, take a leap of faith and devote myself even further to the project.

I recalibrated my commitment to photobooths, through thick and thin, I was going to stick by them.

I made it to my hostel right at 11 o'clock.

After fleeing Russia for Manchuria in 1921, Anatol likely did not get to see his father again. By 1927, Stalin was in power and Anatol's family told him to stop sending letters, for fear that they were under surveillance.

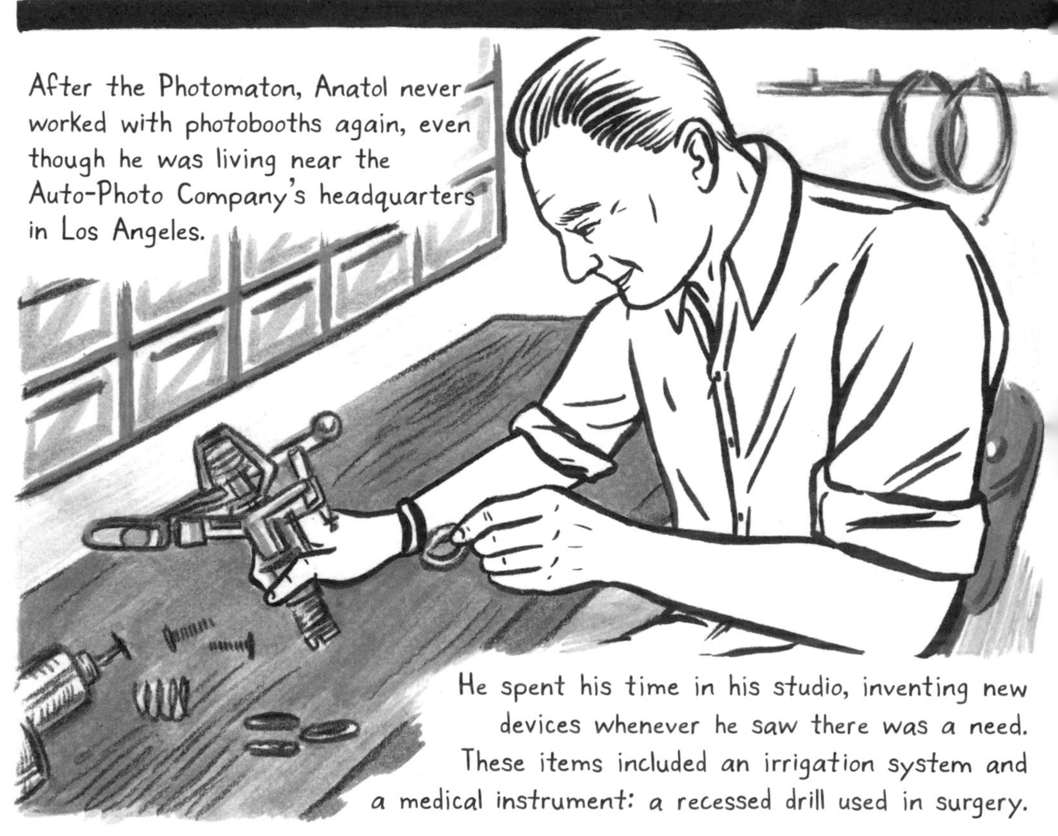

Ganna passed away in 1978. Anatol had been in good health but then had multiple, small strokes. He wasn't the same without Ganna. In 1980, at the age of 86, he passed away from complications related to his heart problems.

Today, Anatol Josepho is not a widely known figure, but he is fondly remembered by some for his determination, his ingenuity and for his generous heart.

I had tried to arrange interviews with key people in Italy, but I had some trouble because of my language barrier and because I didn't realize that nearly everyone goes on vacation in August.

Dedem is a photobooth company based in Rome. They were established in 1962 and are affiliated with (but separate from) Photo-Me International. Their booths, which are all digital now, are in Italy, Spain, Israel and Romania.

I wasn't able to schedule a meeting with anyone from Dedem, so I decided not to go to Rome.

After much ado, I finally arrived in Florence and I fell in love with the city.

I had a couple of restful days to walk around, see some art, eat lots of gelato and use a couple of chemical photobooths.

In Florence, I met Matteo, the man behind Fotoautomatica. We talked about his artisanal photobooth refurbishing business.

He's collected dozens of old booths, salvaged parts from their rusted interiors and in a Frankensteinesque way, created some stunningly simple new machines.

Matteo finds old dip'n'dunk booths in Hungary, Slovakia, Albania, Romania and Bulgaria. The booths are not expensive but there are tariffs to bring them into Italy.

Each booth takes many hours of restoration. He even created his own "secret recipe" of chemicals for photo development.

Fotoautomatica is slowly expanding to other Italian cities. By occupation Matteo is a set designer, the business is a side project. I admired his passion, eye for detail and work ethic.

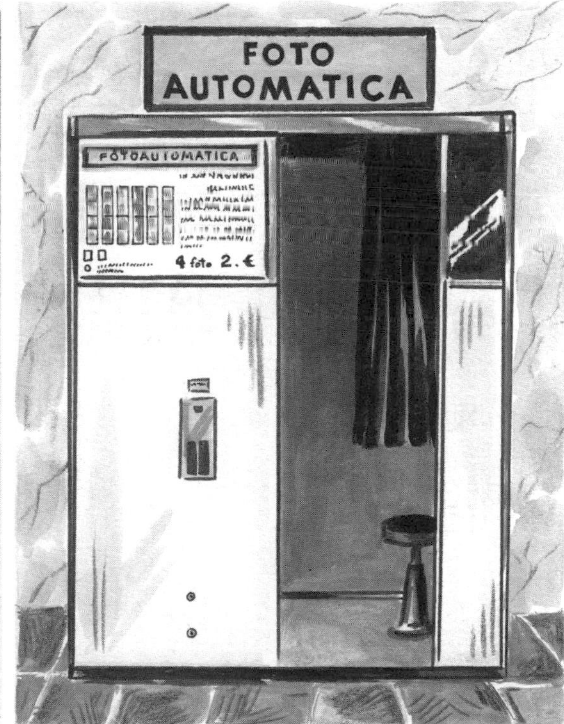

One of his booths at via del Proconsolo.

-ACTIVE-

I had a couple days to fill because I wasn't going to Rome. So upon a friend's recommendation I went to a small town near the Mediterranean sea, Cesena.

Marco and Michele had bought a Model 14 from Auto-Photo Canada for the studio.

Cristina gave me a handful of euros so I could use the photobooth while everyone at the studio was working.
That night they took me out to dinner in the mountains. The food, the wine and the ambience were all amazing.
PHOTOS
PHOTOS
4
POSES
3
3€
After dinner we stopped by the studio and played around in the photobooth, attempting crazy acrobatic poses and fast transitions with all four of us.
Marco asked if he could photograph me the next morning. I agreed but felt a blend of confusion and flattery, he is a very high-profile photographer and not in short supply of models.

The next morning, I arrived at the studio, expecting it to be busy like the day before, but everyone had cleared out of the photography area. Later I found out that Marco had rescheduled a work shoot to photograph me.
During the shoot, his assistant came in to confirm that he would not be able to photograph Bill Clinton during his visit to Italy, Marco was already booked that weekend.
WHAT?! He's too busy to photograph a President but has time to shoot me?
The entire shoot, Marco showered me with compliments.
Oh, thanks, but I'm not beautiful or exotic. I'm just a normal person from Canada.
Your hands have so much personality!
Most of his compliments were thoughtful and specific.

Marco edited the pictures soon after the shoot. They are captivating and the lighting is expertly considered, though it felt odd to see myself through his eyes.

I didn't see myself in the pictures.

I've taken thousands of self-portraits, the photographer-less camera of the photobooth can genuinely capture me.

Before leaving Cesena, we took some photobooth photos. Marco tried to kiss me but I insisted that he not.

In an awkward and joking way I told him that I don't kiss people in photobooths anymore.

Which was true, but it was a fairly recent rule.

In the recent years, I had casually dated a few people but I hadn't been in a relationship since 2009. When I flipped through my photobooth albums and sporadically saw kissing photos, I felt it inaccurately reflected my life as a mainly single person.
I have photos of myself kissing people on first dates who later became just friends and conversely, I've been in love with people that I never got a chance to use a booth with.
Photobooths had documented almost a decade of my life and yet they had not captured the reality of my love life.
Abstaining from kissing in pictures felt like the right thing at the time.

I left Cesena for Milan but I had to transfer in Bologna, I had an hour long wait in the train station.

The attention and affection that Marco had directed at me was beginning to get under my skin.

He proposed that I stay in Italy and live with him in his beautiful house on the Mediterranean sea. I declined.

Later, I found out that he spent hours translating my blog and knew of my project before I arrived in Cesena.

At first, what bothered me about Marco's adoration was that it reminded me of what was missing in my last relationship. My ex in Halifax seldom complimented me. He was loveable but clueless, forgetting things like my birthday and my going-away party.
After some time, I felt indignation that Marco liked me *because* of my work with photobooths. That passion was sacred to me. I was like a monk, devoted and chaste.
YOU CAN'T SEXUALIZE A MONK!
HOW DARE HE LIKE ME?
I WANT TO go HOME!
I felt claustrophobic in the crowded station. I needed to be alone.
I spotted a digital photobooth.
I closed the curtain and started to sob.

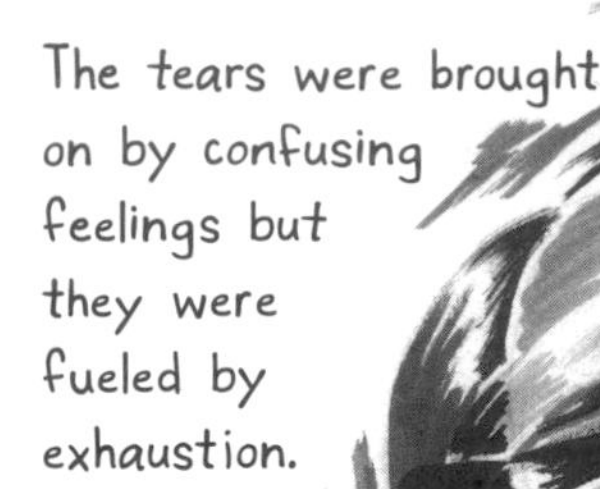

The tears were brought on by confusing feelings but they were fueled by exhaustion.

The photobooth, despite being digital, served as a confessional, a safe, sacred space to divulge my feelings.

I was hot, I was sweaty, I was lugging around all those stupid, heavy books.

In that moment, I could not have been more grateful for the privacy.

I took some passport photos.

>>>>>>>>>>>>> After two days in Milan, I headed home.

FOTOTESSERE
VALIDE PER
foto
per documenti
GRANDE NOVITÀ
Foto multidocumento
5 EURO
2 EURO
For Info
foto
DIGITAL
BOLONGA
TRAIN STATION

PART III

31
When I got back to Halifax, I had just a couple of weeks to finish up all my projects, pack up my life and say goodbye to my friends.
FRAGILE
I arrived in Chicago with so much excitement, energy and gratitude for the experiences I was about to have.
Fortunately, because Chicago is like improv's mecca, I already had some good friends in the city who helped me get settled in.
Within 72 hours I had a transit pass, an American cellphone, and incredibly, an affordable and cute apartment with awesome roommates in the Ukrainian Village.

Anthony, who I met at the International Photobooth Convention, made me feel very welcome at A&A Studios, which is exactly my vision of an ideal creative space.

It's comprised of a shared office, a woodshop, the basement where many photobooth parts are stored, and a showroom, which houses a working Model 11.

I was there as an artist in residence but I also hoped to learn how to service a photobooth. I wanted to learn firsthand what Evelyn and Jocelyn said about a technician's code of honour.

It was an exciting place to show up every day. I just felt like I belonged there with all the other collectors and specialists.

My apartment was only twenty minutes away from the studio on the bus, but many mornings I chose to run because I liked looking at the architecture along the way. The autumn colours made everything seem more beautiful.
R SHOP
Compared to tiny Halifax, the variety of restaurants, cinema, theatre and museums made me feel like the luckiest woman alive.
I was cocooned in culture and I took advantage of it as much as possible. I connected with old friends and made new ones.
Best of all, my close friend Elizabeth, from my high school improv team, was living in Chicago too.

During my first week, I went with Rob, one of the A&A employees, to do the weekly service job on a chemical photobooth at the Empty Bottle, a bar and music venue.

I put my sewing, painting and design skills to use and helped the studio with some custom photobooth projects.

I hand painted all the signage on the interior door, on the stool and on the booth's topper, and designed the signage that wrapped around the sides of the Model 11, all of it looking as original as possible.

I sourced photostrips from the 50s to go on the booth. I also included a strip of myself, so that I could say that I've been in a movie with Robert DeNiro and Morgan Freeman.

"LAST VEGAS"
FILM PROP – *MODEL 11* REPLICA

Shortly after getting settled in Chicago, I got a phone call from my friend, Tyler, who's place I had stayed in Los Angeles. We hadn't spoken since May when we met up in Halifax so he could give me his keys. Apparently my enthusiasm for photobooths had left an impression on him.

I wasn't striving to be an actress but the opportunity sounded like too much fun to pass up.

The production flew me to Toronto and put me up in a nice hotel downtown. So far on my photobooth expedition, I had slept on plenty of couches, stayed in quaint guest rooms and in questionable hostels but, until now, I had never stayed in a spacious hotel room.

The experience marked a big switch for me.

Instead of paying to travel for my photobooth work, *I was getting paid.*

We shot over several days and I had a tremendous amount of fun with the cast and crew.

We used one of my actual albums of photobooth pictures as a prop, my character was also a collector.

Photo prop from the film of my co-star and I.

32

Back in Chicago, I had free reign over the Model 11 to experiment and take as many pictures as I needed, as long as I serviced it and treated it with care.

Anthony showed me how to use colour chemistry in the Model 11. Like most dip'n'dunks it was only ever intended to run B&W chemistry.

The colour photos a Model 11 can produce are gorgeous. They are incredibly detailed but still feel soft and timeless.

With access to the camera, paper and chemistry, there were endless ways that I could manipulate my photos. I tested numerous techniques and gradually learned how to produce the exact effects I wanted.

The rounded back of the Model 11 allowed me to lean far back into the curve, putting more space between me and the camera than I could normally achieve in a photobooth. I could fit more in the frame, that extra space became key in my compositions.

With all the test strips, my collection was growing very quickly. It became a huge chore to log them into my binder system.

The individual photostrips became less precious because I didn't have to pay for each one.

But as a whole, my new photos were a huge development for me. In just a few weeks I had tested out more techniques than I had in the previous nine years.

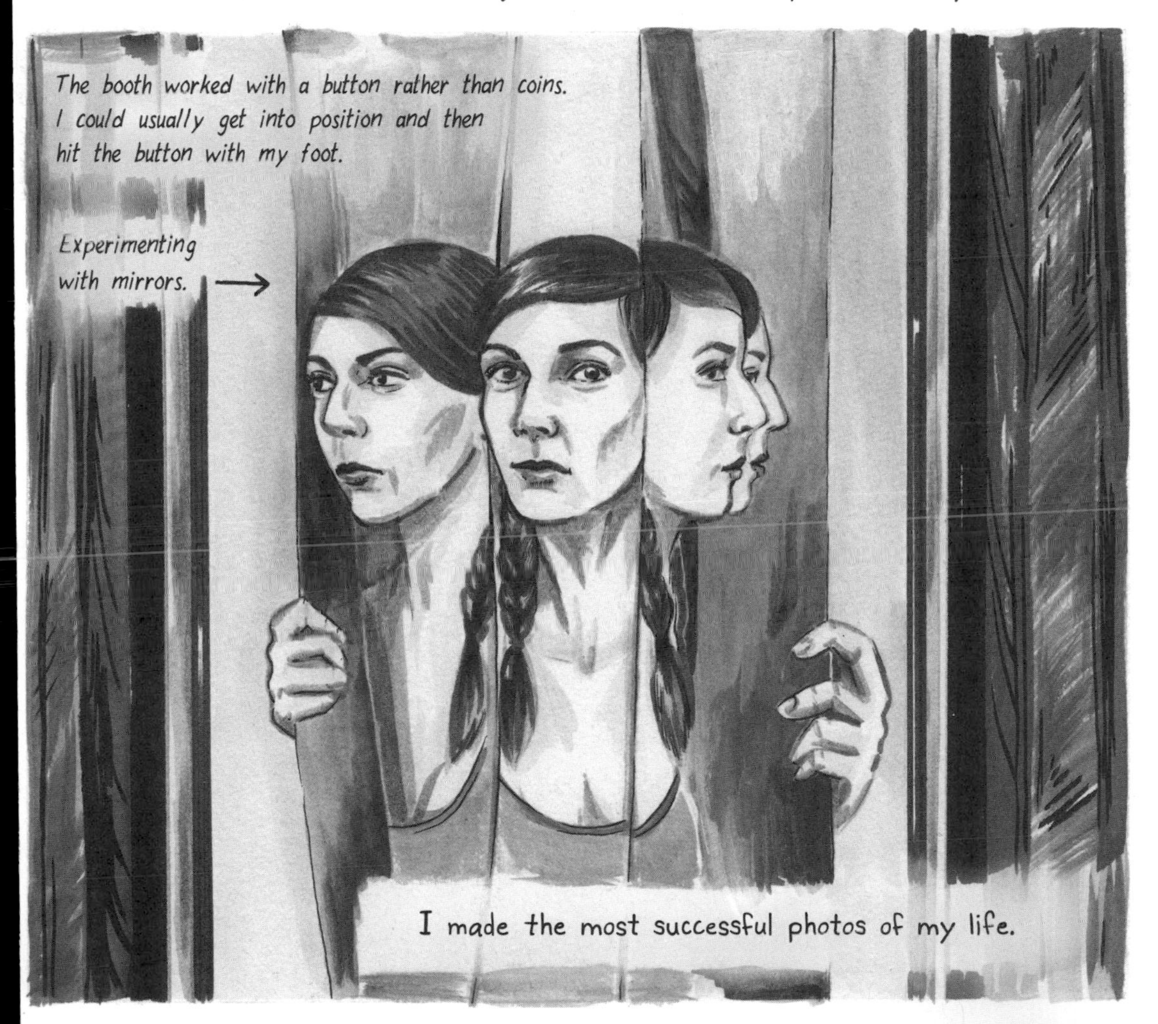

After the first month, I knew that Model 11, in and out.

When I used it, it felt like I was collaborating with a friend.

Just by listening to its sounds I knew where in the development process it was.

I knew its timing between frames.

I knew how its flashes would hit the angles of my face.

I knew exactly where to stand to create the focus I desired.

With styled hair and make up, using two mirrors at an angle.

I placed red acetate with circle cutout on camera lens to create a soft glow on the edges. Turned the camera's aperature up to let in more light. Placed magnifying plastic on the door's glass. Held hands six inches from glass and angled them up to catch the flash above.

I knew everything about it but I also felt like it knew everything about me. Like the perfect partner, meeting all my needs.

I lined the booth →
with black fabric so the
mirror would only catch
my reflection. Bent plexi
glass mirror to elongate
reflection.
← I placed horizontal
bands of coloured acetate
across the glass to create
a gradient, going from
blue tint at top to red
at bottom.
← Testing out patterned
paper backgrounds.
The relationship felt more nourishing
and meaningful than what I had had
with any of my romantic partners
in recent years.

With all that I had learned, I felt inspired to shoot another stop motion animation.

I decided to make it more frames per second and longer than the others I had made before.

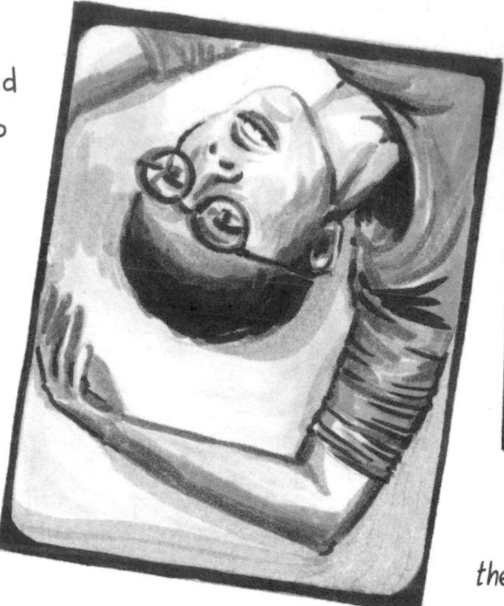

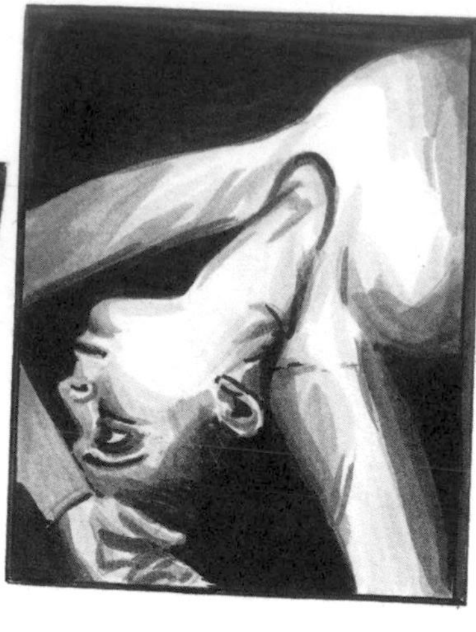

I spent a few weeks testing out the props and rehearsing my poses.

Because I was starring in the animation, I needed to stay in position between taking strips. So I asked my friends, Elizabeth and Rachel, to assist me by collecting the photostrips as they came out, pushing the button to trigger the camera, changing out the filters on the glass and manipulating the props.

It took eight hours to shoot, and later, one hundred hours to edit. I named it *LaCuna.*

A&A
A&A STUDIOS
CHICAGO
active

33

Surrounded all day by vintage photographs at the studio, I felt inspired to buy some online for myself.

Quick searches revealed a sizeable market for vintage photobooth pictures.

I started following auctions that I wasn't bidding in and noted which characteristics sold for the highest prices.

I learned the nuances of the market and spent a lot of money in the process too.

I wistfully watched many photos I sought after go way above my price point and I bitterly lost other auctions to sneaky last second bids by other collectors.

Social media has made it relatively easy for these collectors to find each other and share their images. The market is evolving into a community.

Online, I met Seth, a collector in Massachusetts.

His primary collection consists of stereoviews and other forms of 3D photography. He only recently started to collect photobooth pictures and he thinks the appeal is that each photo is unique.

Seth believes that the market for photobooth pictures is less developed than for older forms of vintage photography like daguerreotypes, tintypes and cabinet cards.

I contacted Albert, one of the top online sellers of photobooth pictures. Since 2007 he's been regularly going to flea markets, antique stores, and estate sales.

Selling photographs is his side business and he sees it as part of a larger preservation effort. He wants photographs that would otherwise be discarded to have a new life.

I think that Albert has been so successful because he sees himself as an intermediary between collectors and photos. When photos that he's sold appear in publications or in artwork, he's personally delighted.

Add to favorite sellers

Items for sale

Feedback ratings

★★★★★ 481	Item as described	1,060	0
★★★★★ 477	Communication	Positive	Neutral
★★★★★ 480	Shipping time		
★★★★★ 481	Shipping charges		

Member since Nov 18, 2007 | United States

Albert senses that buyers are competitive with one another but that generally photobooth collectors are more lighthearted than other types of photo collectors. Over the years he's formed friendships the most serious collectors.

On average his photobooth pictures sell for $12-$14, though there are exceptions. Once a photo sold for $400!

Albert has observed that it's getting harder to find vintage photos at flea markets, which will likely impact the market in coming years.

I started a modest collection of vintage photobooth pictures. I was curious to meet more dealers and collectors but I sensed their story is large enough for its own book.

One of A&A's projects was for a Tiki-themed restaurant in Minneapolis.

I painted a Tiki mask and we wired the eyes to glow red. The photos come out the mask's mouth. The booth had been a chemical machine but the team converted it to digital.

Two staff were needed to drive the seven hours to Minneapolis to unload it. Rob was a pro at unloading heavy booths and could drive the big truck. I was clearly the second strongest person at the studio, so I went with him.

It was October and the 2012 Election was in full swing. America was at its most American.

When I got to my room, I plopped on the bed. The room was non-smoking but it smelt like that designation had only been a suggestion. I turned on the television, watched the Presidential debate and ate some cold fried chicken.

The next morning we installed the Tiki booth at the restaurant. We got some help from the restaurant staff.

Rob drove back to Chicago but I hung back so I could interview Todd Erickson, a photobooth veteran in St. Paul.

In 1978 Todd bought an arcade games and amusement company from his uncle. Today his primary business is photobooth rentals.

I visited him in his warehouse filled with dozens and dozens of old and dusty arcade games.

 Todd is obsessed with producing the highest quality photos possible. 

He believes that digital booths are junk and that PC computers just aren't reliable. Over the years he's seen many digital models come only to go to the landfill a few years later. In contrast, he has chemical machines that have taken over *one million* strips over their lifetimes!

As Todd explained his mechanical approach he used a lot of terms I didn't understand. A lot of what he said might as well have been gibberish to me.

He was flabbergasted when I told him that I'd never worked on a motor or transmission.

Clearly, I had a lot left to learn.

35

After visiting Todd's warehouse, I felt motivated to learn more about the inner workings of the photobooth.

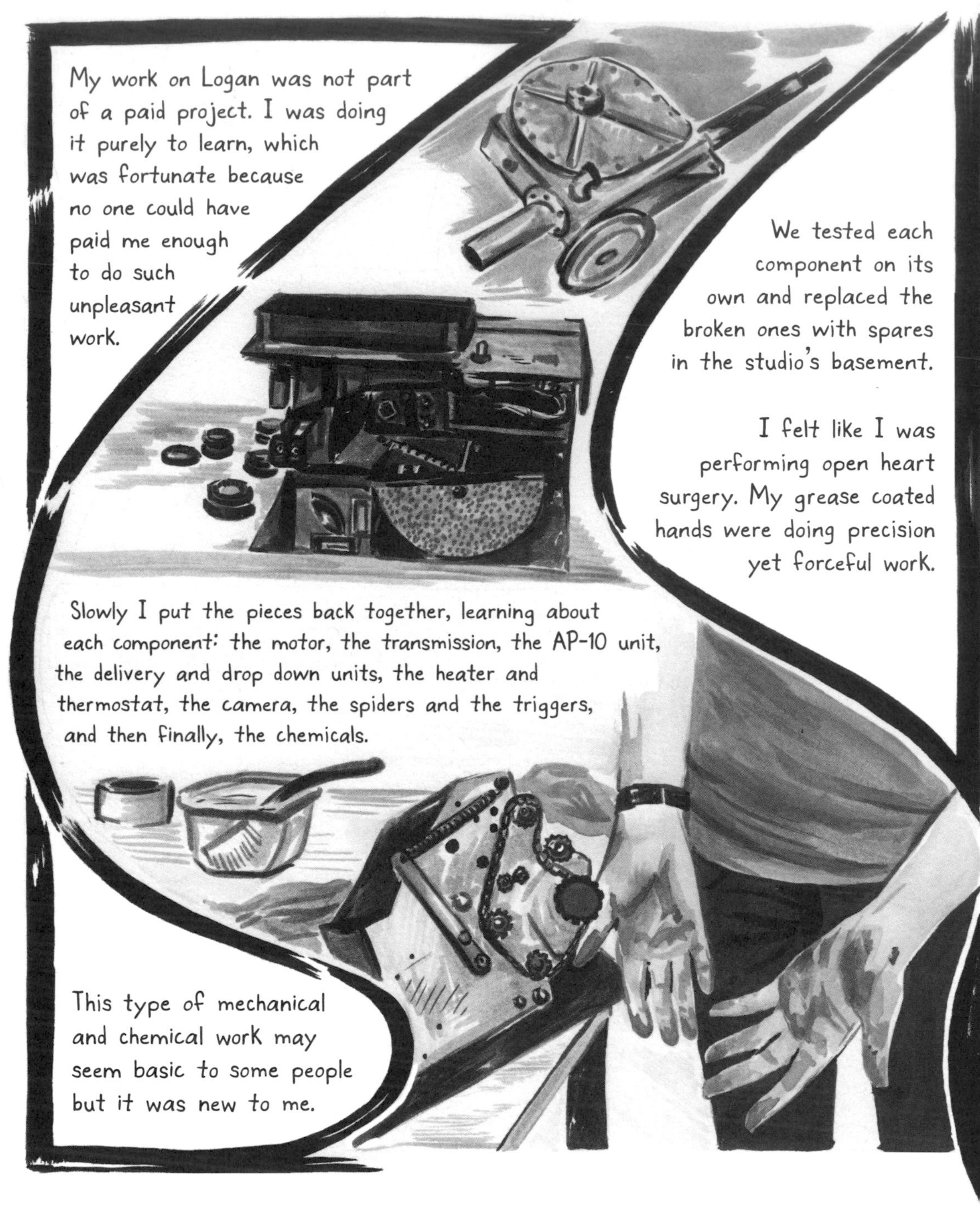

I hardly took any science classes in high school. Instead, my schedule was filled with specialized arts classes. I felt so empowered doing this type of physical work. In a short period I filled large gaps in my knowledge of how stuff actually works.

I felt deeply conflicted about advocating for the continued existence of chemical photobooths when I could see so plainly that they can be seriously harmful.

We got Logan up and running on colour chemistry. Instead of putting a back on him and enclosing the booth, we took advantage of his openness.

We tested the booth's capabilities for full length photos. The flash couldn't extend that far so we set up additional lights further away from the booth.

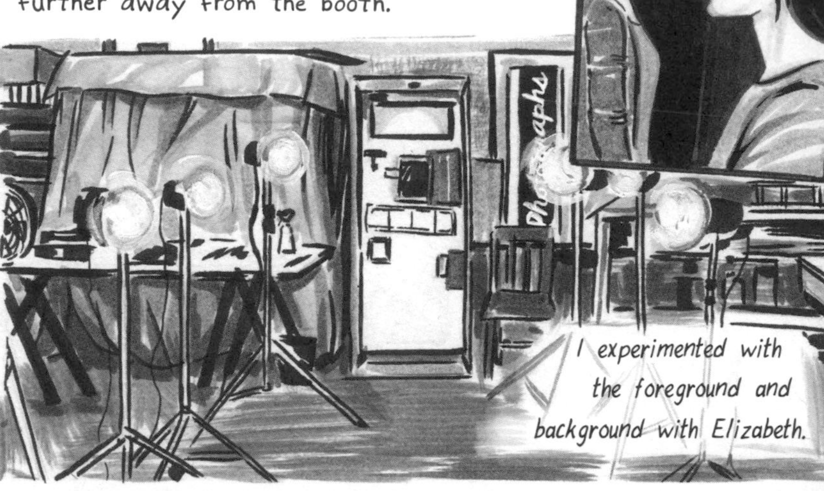

I experimented with the foreground and background with Elizabeth.

Chicago has an incredible comics arts scene. I visited Quimby's Bookstore regularly for their great selection and because they have a chemical booth, a Model 21!

One day, I took some photos while I shopped for comics. Listening to the booth running, I could tell it was unwell. My photos came out okay but I diagnosed the problem as being in the motor.

I spoke with the staff, the booth had been having some trouble. We talked over some solutions.

My new found knowledge had already proven to be useful out in the field!

Chicago

QUIMBY'S
BOOKSTORE

36
In mid-November I made a trip to New York City.
Just like when I was in Los Angeles, all my plans went off without a hitch and luck was always in my favour.
I stayed with friends of friends in Midtown, right beside Central Park.
One morning I visited the artist Herman Costa in his charming apartment.
In 1968, as a young man, Herman moved to New York City and found a job as a textile designer. In his words, that was "the year that the world changed from black and white to colour."
PLAYLAND
WE BUY & SELL
US & FOREGIN
COINS
Boutique
Sol
FINEST PLAYLAND IN NEW YORK
1 HR
Herman always lived or worked within one block from an arcade or a Woolworth's variety store, which always housed a photobooth.
He witnessed radical changes all around him and began to photograph himself and his eclectic friends for a quarter a piece.

In 1974 he had his first photobooth art show of 300 single strips, which was followed by an article about him in the *Village Voice* where he was deemed "The King of the Photobooth."

One day he saw a technician servicing a booth. He rushed home, grabbed his art portfolio and rushed back. The technician was impressed by his art and invited him to come to Auto-Photo's warehouse in Queens.

Alberto Caroselli worked for Auto-Photo and later became the President of the American Division when they were bought by Photo-Me.

Alberto was like Herman's fairy godfather, letting him take free photos and delivering photobooths to galleries whenever Herman had an art show.

Herman started to create larger compositions by placing the strips side by side. The strips were always uncut because the intact strip was a record of the time that has passed, it elevated the artform.

In all Herman's works you can see his love of prints and patterns and of fashion and costumes.

Art directors began to take notice and Herman's work went mainstream. He was commissioned by major publications to make portraits of celebrities.

Herman shot Mike Myers for Seventeen magazine in 1988.

In 1986, the Museum of Modern Art bought and exhibited a piece of his for their permanent collection.

In 1992, MTV commissioned Herman to make a promotional image for their *Rock the Vote, Choose or Lose* campaign. By assembling many photostrips, Herman made an expansive, fluttering American flag.

MTV invited the three Presidential candidates to appear on *Rock the Vote.* George Bush Sr. and Ross Perot declined, but Bill Clinton agreed and stood in front of Herman's artwork for millions to see.

Herman stopped taking photobooth pictures in the late 90s when the booths began to disappear, but his work continued to be exhibited and collected.

Herman and I had only planned to have lunch together but I stayed until long after dark. I could have listened to his stories for many more hours.

At the end of my trip, I met with Abie, a technician for Classic Photobooth, whose headquarters are in Seattle. Abie was born and raised in New York and is an art school graduate. If anyone understands what it is to be ahead of the trends, it is her.

Abie's got gold-plated teeth.

When she first took this job in 2009, a large part of the work was finding new bars and clubs in which to place booths but she soon discovered how difficult that was in NYC.

Square footage is so precious that venues don't have the extra space for a photobooth. A couple of extra tables and chairs in that same space would generate more revenue.

Abie thinks that NYC goes through trends so much faster than any other American city. Photobooths were part of a retro American trend that peaked in NYC in 2004/05 and then became mainstream everywhere else.

Abie observed a lot of nightlife while on the job. She said that most people who go out are 21-23 years old. So people who were 21 in 2005 may still like classic American novelties but today's 21 year olds don't relate to that trend.

As Abie sees it, chemical photobooths are already passé, for the second time.

PHOTOBOOTH
ACTIVE
ACE HOTEL
NEW YORK CITY

I was so sure that people would use chemical booths more often if only they knew they were disppearing.

April 26th seemed like a fitting day, selfishly because it's my birthday but it's also the birthday of three other key individuals.*

A quick search revealed that April 26th is already "Pretzel Day."

If pretzels merit their own day, then so do photobooths. They can share the date.

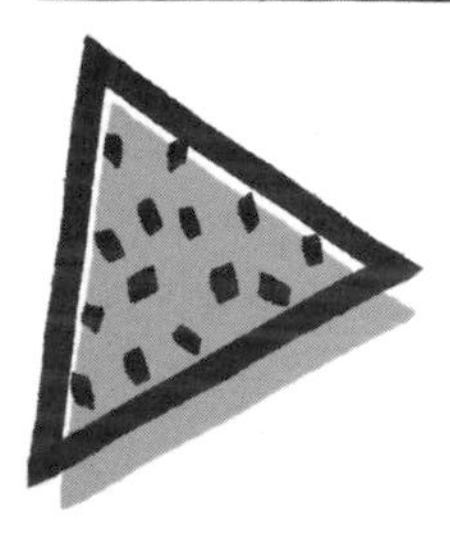

But I knew that petitioning for the recognition of *Use a Vintage Photobooth Day* would not ultimately be the best way to protect this endangered species. I would have to start making the book that I pledged to make when I launched my Photobooth Expedition fundraiser nine months earlier.

* *Henry Morgenthau Sr., Tim Garrett and Jeff Grostern.*

37

I had one last person to visit before I could say my Photobooth Expedition was over. I headed to Burlington, Vermont.

Nakki Goranin spent many years traveling the U.S. collecting every shred of information she could find on the old photobooth companies.

She has completely devoted her life to her research, her collections and to her fine art photography.

In 2008, her book *American Photobooth* was published.

American Photobooth stands out from the few photobooth books that came before it and the few that have come since because Nakki is more than just a photo collector, she is a scholar.

Nakki is likely the world's most knowledgeable person on the subject of photobooth history.

She owns three booths, a Model 14, a Deluxe Photomatic and a hand built, wooden booth from the 1930s.

I was thrilled to meet her and see some rare pieces in her collection. We talked non-stop for two days.

Looking at hundreds of photos from the past, you are reminded of your own legacy.

Nakki is the only child of two only children. She has no aunts, uncles or cousins. Her parents have both passed away and she has no children. She kept telling me that she saw her younger self in me. It gave me pause.

The photobooth community is one way that Nakki creates these family ties. I gained a better understanding of the importance of sharing a common interest with others.

And it made me consider my level of devotion to photobooths.

Nakki is writing several other books on the history of photography, eventually she plans on leaving her collections to the Smithsonian for others to appreciate, which seems like a rich legacy to me, but it's not necessarily the path I'd like follow.

I had already begun to feel glimmers of resentment towards photobooths, for all that I had forgone to be with them. I was afraid that feeling would grow.

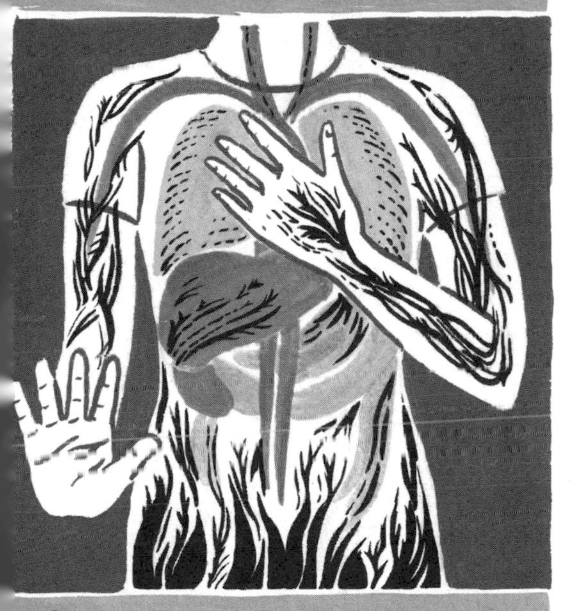

Photobooths and I had been on a long honeymoon, but our relationship had evolved. It was more complex now.

Back in Chicago, I went to A&A to gather my things. It was a Saturday and I was the only one there.

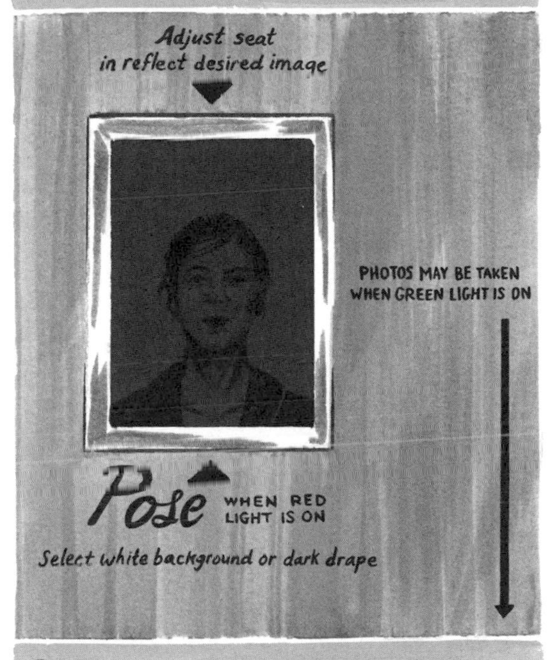

I took a few last strips in the Model 11. Logan didn't have any chemicals in him, but I said goodbye to him too.

The winter holidays were fast approaching and I was going back to Edmonton to be with my family. My big, awesome family, who I missed very much.

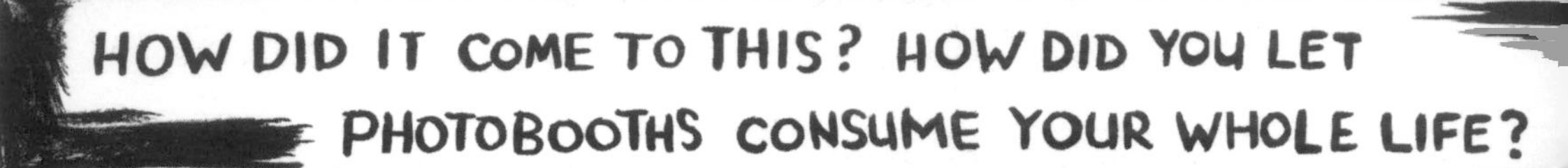
HOW DID IT COME TO THIS? HOW DID YOU LET PHOTOBOOTHS CONSUME YOUR WHOLE LIFE?

HOW MUCH TIME DO YOU NEED TO MAKE THIS BOOK?
DO YOU THINK A BOOK COULD REALLY CHANGE THE COURSE OF THEIR FATE?
WHY WOULD YOU INVEST IN SOMETHING THAT IS ALREADY ON THE BRINK OF EXTINCTION?
IF YOU CAN'T ANSWER THAT THEN MAYBE YOU SHOULDN'T INVEST ANYMORE TIME INTO THIS CAUSE.
YOU'RE SETTING YOURSELF UP TO BE REALLY SAD WHEN THEY DO GO.

I don't know. I have other hobbies, other collections that I wish I had time for.

I'm not sure, I've never made a book before. Maybe I could write and illustrate it in a year if I didn't do much else.

Realistically, probably not. But I want to give people a chance to respond, to know that they're going before they're gone.

I don't have a rational answer for that.

When you love something, you can't just choose not to feel that way anymore.

My urge to promote their cause isn't even a passion anymore, it's just innate.

I know.

I felt like I chose to love these things that couldn't really love me back, not because they're inanimate, but because they're just too preoccupied with their own extinction.
I would have lots of time in the coming months to reflect on this.
$1
LOG
Photographs
I had prioritized photobooths over many of my relationships, but in turn, new friendships grew from within the community.
My life was so much richer for it.
Leaving Chicago, I was overcome with gratitude. I knew that it didn't really matter what happened next because everything had already been worthwhile.

A new, quiet chapter was about to begin.

Acknowledgments

Thanks to:

- My loving parents, my marvelous siblings and to my incredible extended family for their endless support and understanding. Extra thanks to my sister Eryn!
- Everyone who donated to my Photobooth Expedition fundraiser in the spring of 2012. This book started with that support and boost of encouragement.
- Those who hosted me during my travels, especially Corbin and Paul in Venice, Marion in Paris and Elizabeth in Burlington.
- Everyone interviewed and featured in this book for welcoming me into your lives.
- Andy Brown for taking a chance on this project.
- The Alberta Foundation for the Arts for its financial support.
- Brian Meacham, Tim Garrett and to everyone who's contributed to Photobooth.net over the years. The rich databases were incredible resources while researching this book.
- The Josepho family, especially Sharon Josepho for sharing her family's story with me.
- Nakki Goranin for her wealth of knowledge and openness to sharing ideas.
- Georgia Webber for being a trusted source of comics feedback.
- To my friends who have been there for me at different stages of this process, especially Krista, Kory, Elizabeth, Lisa and Solomon.
- Librarians and library staff everywhere.

SELECTED SOURCES

Boyle, Bern, and Linda Duchin. *Photomaton: A Contemporary Survey of Photobooth Art.* Rochester, NY: Pyramid Arts Center, 1987. Print.

Bal, Mieke. "Telling Objects: A Narrative Perspective on Collecting." *The Cultures of Collecting.* Eds. John Elsner and Roger Cardinal. London: Reaktion Books, 1994. 97-115. Print.

Chéroux, Clément, Anne Lacoste and Sam Stourdzé, eds. *Derriere le Rideau: L'Esthétique Photomaton.* Lausaune: Musée de L'Élysée; Arles: Éditions Photosynthèses, 2012.

Goranin, Nakki. *American Photobooth.* New York City: W. W. Norton & Company, 2008. Print.

Klevian, Birna. "Regarding the Photobooth." *Katalos: Journal of Photography and Video.* Vol.12 No.3 (2000): 3-21. Print.

Pellicer, Raynal. *Photobooth: Art of the Automatic Portrait.* Trans. Anthony Shugaar. New York City: Harry N. Abrams, 2010. Print.

Simkin, David. "Automatic Portrait Photography." *Brighton Early 20th-Century Photography.* Sussex Photo History, August 2005. Web. accessed on January 1, 2013.

Other sources for this book include articles in the archives of *The New York Times*, the *Boston Globe*, the *Los Angeles Times* and the *Chicago Tribune.* Also consulted were the United States Census records, the United States Patent and Trademark Office, the Canadian Patents Database and ancestry websites. Ephemera, such as advertisements and technician's manuals were also collected from photobooth companies.

Specific magazines articles referenced or represented in this book are cited in text or in the Notes and Citations section.

NOTES AND CITATIONS

Many historical images were collected and used as reference material for the illustrations in this book. Most often, multiple images were consulted to composite a new view of the subject. At times, multiple sources could not be found and one primary image was used for reference. In those instances the owner of the image is cited according to page number.

The vintage photobooth photographs drawn in this book belong to my personal collection, with the exception of historical images such as those of Anatol Josepho and the members of the Surrealist movement. The rights to the photobooth art represented in this book belong to the respective artists.

---

p. 3- Meags is pronounced "Megz."

p. 16- If a model number is followed by a C or P it operates as a Colour or New Processor.

p. 19- Colour photostrips typically have a thick white border. B&W photostrips typically have a thin black border.

p. 21- The locations and statuses listed on the "Photobooth Portraits" throughout this book were accurate at the time of publication but are likely to change in the future. The portraits from pages 39 to 99 are historical booths that I did not personally visit. The portraits from pages 109 to 263 are booths that I used.

p. 26- Photo reference from the collection of Deutsches Museum in Munich was used for the Bosco Automal.

p. 27- Photo reference from the collection of Roger Viollet was use for the Automatic Photographic Device.

p. 29- Anatol Josepho's birth place is most often cited as Omsk, Siberia. This error originated in an article published in 1928. The family confirms he was born in Tomsk, a smaller town in the same region.

p. 33- Headline referenced is from *The New York Times*, August 2, 1914.

p. 38- The wedding illustration of Anatol and Ganna was fabricated based on trends from that period. The Josepho family does not believe they took an official wedding photo. The ceremony was likely a small, non-religious event.

p. 46- Photo reference from the *Boston Daily Globe*, August 30, 1927 was used for the photo-booth pictures of Anatol and Henry Morgenthau Sr.

p. 46- Article referenced is from *Modern Mechanics* magazine, November 1928.

p. 47- The paper bond for the Société Continentale Photomaton belongs to my collection.

p. 47- Photo reference from the Archive of Prussian Cultural Heritage was used for the Berlin Photomaton studio.

p. 49- Photo reference from a Woolworth's promotional item (date unknown) was used for the Photomaton advertisement.

p. 49- Photo reference from the collection of Nakki Goranin, as published in *American Photobooth* was used for the Photomovette advertisement.

p. 50- Photo reference from the archives of the Société Continentale Photomaton was used for the Miss Photomaton advertisement.

p. 50- Photo reference from the *Evening Post*, Wellington, New Zealand, January 23, 1940 was used for the advertisement.

p. 56- Article referenced is from *Modern Mechanix* magazine, November 1936. No author is listed.

p. 57- Photo reference from *Modern Mechanix* magazine, November 1936 was used for the advertisement.

p. 74- Quote by Peter Egan is from "Still Life, With Yellow Sting Ray," an article from September 2010 on the website RoadTrack.com.

p. 81-85- Photo references from *Toronto Star*, April 14, 1928 and from *Photographic Canadiana*, May-June 2007 were used for the Phototeria.

p. 83- Headline referenced is from the *Herald Examiner*, Chicago, February 15, 1929.

p. 83- Article referenced is from the *Free Lance Star*, Virginia, February 10, 1959.
p. 88- The rights holder for the portrait of Salvador Dali and Gala is unknown.

p. 86- Photo reference from the Société des Auteurs dans les Arts Graphiques et Plastiques was used for the portrait of Yves Tanguy.

p. 86- Photo reference from the collection of the Centre Pompidou was used for the portrait of Marie Berthe Aurenche.

p. 88- Photo reference from the collection of the Centre Pompidou was used for *La Revolution Surrealist.*

p. 89- Photo reference for the cover of *Variétés* was found on an auction website. The quote is not attributed to an author. The translation to English is by Anthony Shugaar and appears in *Photobooth: The Art of the Automatic Portrait.*

p. 89- Cover of *Time* magazine was from the week of January 29, 1965.

p. 93- Photo reference from the collection of Nakki Goranin, as published in *American Photobooth* was used for the Phota-Strip Junior advertisement.

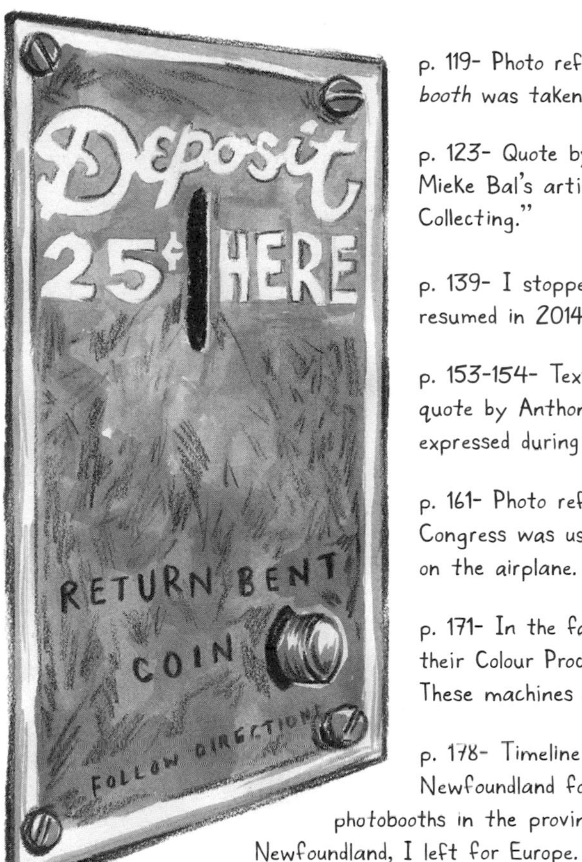

p. 119- Photo reference of the artists of *Concerning the Photobooth* was taken by Stuart McIntyre.

p. 123- Quote by Susan M. Pearce appears on page 12 of Mieke Bal's article "Telling Objects: A Narrative Perspective on Collecting."

p. 139- I stopped performing improv for several years, but resumed in 2014.

p. 153-154- Text within the quotation marks is not a direct quote by Anthony Vizzari, rather a summary of his opinions expressed during our interview.

p. 161- Photo reference from the collection of the U.S. Library of Congress was used for the image of Will Rogers and Wiley Post on the airplane.

p. 171- In the fall of 2013 Auto-Photo Canada began converting their Colour Processor machines to operate with B&W chemistry. These machines are being sold to European small businesses.

p. 178- Timeline note: after my trip to Montreal, I visited Newfoundland for two weeks. I tracked and used all the chemical photobooths in the province. A few days after returning from Newfoundland, I left for Europe.

p. 182- Photo reference from the collection of the Centre Pompidou was used for the portrait of Paul Éluard.

p. 216- The letter written by Société Continentale Photomaton was first published in *Conversations secrètes des Français sous l'Occupation*, by Antoine Lefébure, 1993. The English translation was done by Anthony Shugaar.

p. 219- Photo reference from the collection of the Josepho family was used for the portrait of Anatol and Ganna.

p. 234- Timeline note: After leaving Halifax, before arriving in Chicago, I spent a week in Toronto, making photobooth art with Italian artists.

p. 238- *Last Vegas* was released in November 2013, the photobooth prop can be seen in the opening sequence.

p. 241- The film I starred in will be released in the summer of 2014, at the time of this book's publication it has not yet been named.

p. 252- Every photobooth has a counter which tracks how many strips it has taken.

First English Edition

Edited by Andy Brown for Conundrum Press
Font production by Tracy Hurren

Printed by Gauvin Press in Gatineau, Quebec, Canada

Library and Archives Canada Cataloguing in Publication

Fitzgerald, Meags, 1987-, author, illustrator
Photobooth: a biography / Meags Fitzgerald.

ISBN 978-1-894994-82-8 (pbk.)

1. Photobooths--History--Comic books, strips, etc.
2. Portrait photography--History--Comic books, strips, etc.
3. Self-portraits--History--Comic books, strips, etc.
4. Graphic novels. I. Title.

TR680.F58 2014 779'.2 C2014-900405-2

Conundrum Press
Greenwich, NS, Canada
www.conundrumpress.com

Conundrum Press acknowledges the financial support of the Canada Council for the Arts and the Government of Canada through the Canada Book Fund toward its publishing activities.

Meags Fitzgerald acknowledges the support of the Province of Alberta through the Alberta Foundation for the Arts and would to thank them for their support.